Stay Prepped

10 Steps to Succeeding in College
(And Having a Ball Doing It)

A. Nicki Washington, Ph.D.

Stay Prepped: 10 Steps to Succeeding in College
(And Having a Ball Doing It)
Copyright © 2013
A. Nicki Washington, Ph.D.

ALL RIGHTS RESERVED.

Printed in the United States of America. No portion of this publication may be reproduced, stored in any electronic system, or transmitted in any form or by any means, electronic, mechanical, photocopy, recording, or otherwise, without written permission from the author. Brief quotations may be used in literary reviews.

'A' Game Educational Services

www.preppedforsuccess.com

Cover art by Sara Roney, Sunrise Studios Design and Photography

ISBN: 978-0-9847467-3-6

FOR INFORMATION CONTACT:
A. Nicki Washington, Ph.D.
P.O. Box 101842
Arlington, VA 22210
nicki@preppedforsuccess.com

Acknowledgements

I'd like to thank all of the individuals who inspired this book, including former professors, administrators, students, family, and friends.

This book is dedicated to my parents, who have always supported my efforts in more ways than imaginable. Thank you for simultaneously being my worst critics and biggest fans. I am forever grateful.

TABLE OF CONTENTS

Introduction..7

Step One:
    Learn to Love Your New Home…and All That Comes With It....9

Step Two:
    Have a Resume and Professional Attire..............................23

Step Three:
    Know, Understand, and Remember Registration, Advising, and Graduation Requirements..29

Step Four:
    Your Classes Are Your Priority 39

Step Five:
    Time Management and Study Skills Are Your Best Friends......49

Step Six:
    Search for Financial Aid Until You Have a Zero Balance 57

Step Seven:
    Learn and Practice Money-Management Skills.....................65

Step Eight:
    Participate in Internships, Co-ops, and Other Experiences........75

Step Nine:
    Understand the Road Ahead as a First-Generation College Student...81

Step Ten:
    Take Care of Your Physical and Mental Health 89

Final Thoughts 97

Introduction

This book was several years in the making. I honestly envisioned writing it for the first time in the summer of 2000, immediately following my graduation from Johnson C. Smith University. Over the next few years, I would speak to undergraduates at various colleges about how to be successful in college and beyond. However, life was happening. I was in graduate school, and the thoughts I would jot down would have to wait while I completed classes, internships, research, and my dissertation.

After I began teaching at Howard University, I thought I would be able to pick up where I left off. Once again, life kept happening. I had courses to teach, research to complete, papers and proposals to write, and personal highs and lows. Finally, I realized that life would continue to happen, as long as I'm alive and breathing. I just needed to finish it.

The more important thing I realized was that, over the 13-year span it took me to finally complete this book, not much changed in terms of the issues and topics that college students struggled with. Many students were still making the same mistakes in 2013 that we made in 1996. Sure, there were a few changes, like smartphones, Google, Facebook, tweets, texting, and 24-hour access to technology. However, there were certain things that didn't seem to change with time or technology.

I remember my parents telling me from the time I graduated from high school to the time I graduated from college that those would be the "best four years of your life. You will never have this opportunity again, so make the most of it." How right they were!

My college years were absolutely amazing. I met wonderful, lifelong friends, learned a lot, partied like a rock star, established incredible relationships with people on campus, and took advantage of every opportunity to grow personally and professionally. Like most 18-22-year olds, I had my share of self-induced drama, stress, and issues. However, they were few and far between. Everyone should be so fortunate. Sadly, there are too many college students who aren't. For a number of reasons, their experience includes stress, uncertainty, and emotional rollercoasters, to name a few.

It was my goal to write this book for every student entering or currently enrolled in college. *Prepped for Success* got you *to* college. However, it didn't get you *through* college. So here we are. There are a lot of strategies that helped me succeed as an undergraduate. I've also witnessed the successes and failures of many an undergraduate as a college professor.

The truth is that there is no magic formula to being successful in college. It requires being prepared, proactive, and positive. One of my college basketball coaches would quote the five P's to us weekly: prior preparation prevents poor performance. A major part of your preparation is reading this book. The remainder is implementing the strategies outlined throughout.

Each chapter (except this one and the final thoughts) is a step to help you get closer to your goal. Succeeding in college is about a lot more than simply passing your courses. You will learn as you read that the best college experience is one that allows you to enjoy your new independence and still remain on track to graduate. Despite your classification, you will find most, if not all of the steps beneficial. Remember, you not only want to graduate, but also have wonderful memories to look back upon throughout your life. Good luck!

Step One

Learn to Love Your New Home…and All That Comes With It

Living on campus can be one of the biggest adjustments in college. As an only child, I wasn't used to sharing anything. Whatever was used or misplaced, I was the responsible party. I could eat and go whenever and wherever I wanted, and I was sure that my house (moreso my room) was clean to my standards (even if those were slightly less than my parents'). Simply put, I was comfortable at home. That was my personal space and no one invaded it unless granted permission. That all changed on freshman move-in day.

Imagine forty girls on one floor, sharing two bathrooms with three toilets, showers, and sinks each. In addition, we had no central air conditioning. Did I mention it was August in North Carolina? This was my new home for the next nine months? Suffice it to say I was *not* a happy camper. Once we moved in and unpacked, I begged my parents to let me stay with them at the hotel that night. Of course, that wasn't an option. This was my "we're not in Kansas anymore" moment. I was going to have to adjust and adapt to my new home, and quickly.

My experience isn't uncommon. For most of you, this is your first time away from home. You may be in a new city, state, or country, so it's ok to feel slightly displaced. However, it's important to remember that successfully transitioning to college requires you to successfully transition to living on a college campus. This chapter presents a few things to remember (or learn) in order to better adjust to your new environment.

Give Your New Home a Good Cleaning

The first thing my parents and I did before unpacking was scrub my room from top to bottom. You could smell Lysol and

Mr. Clean throughout the hallway! It was an exhausting task, but I definitely appreciated it afterwards. Unless your residence hall is brand new, your room has been occupied by several students before you. It is best that you thoroughly clean it before unpacking. Remember, you will reside here for the next nine months. Make yourself as comfortable as possible.

Keep Your Own Toiletries and Cleaning Essentials

At some point, the bathroom will run out of toilet tissue, soap, or paper towels. While it's supposed to remain stocked, there is always that awkward moment when you need it and there is none available. To avoid this problem, keep a set of your own necessities in your room. The minimal must-have items to get you through the year include:

- *Disinfectant spray and wipes*
- *Trash can and bags*
- *Toilet tissue*
- *Hand soap and sanitizer*
- *Paper towels*
- *Mattress cover*
- *Laundry detergent and bleach*
- *Bug spray*
- *Alcohol and peroxide*
- *Band-Aids*
- *Broom and dustpan*
- *Cabinet liners*

Most of these items are self-explanatory. Remember, you aren't the first inhabitant. A small trash can limits the type and amount of trash left in the room at any time. Keep a can of unscented bug spray, in case there are any "unwanted guests." You can also spray the perimeter of your room before unpacking, including windows, as a safeguard. A mattress cover will provide a layer of protection between you and the previously used mattress. Before you put it on, make sure you use disinfectant spray to sanitize the mattress. Finally, place cabinet liners in every drawer that will store clothes, toiletries, etc.

Get to Know Your Roommate and Neighbors

Why you would need to know your neighbors when you move into a new house? First, you want to make sure you respect each other and can live together peacefully. Next, you want to know what to expect in your new surroundings. Finally, you want someone that will keep a friendly eye on your house, in the event that you are away. The same things apply in your new dorm. Your roommate is the person you will spend the most time with, so you two must learn to cohabitate. While it's not a requirement, hopefully you can also become friends.

I was fortunate enough to choose my roommate my freshman year. Ebony was the daughter of my parents' college friends. We were both only children, had similar interests, and knew each other from annual family get-togethers. It was the best-case scenario for both of us! My first time away from home, and I was sharing a room with someone that I not only knew, but trusted and liked as well!

Ironically, I've met and worked with many students who chose not to room with friends attending the same college as them. In an attempt to meet new people, they didn't want to stay within their "comfort zone." Be wary of this decision for a few reasons.

One of the great things about college is the opportunity to meet people from different locations, cultures, and backgrounds. This is a wonderful time to embrace differences and enhance your social knowledge outside of the classroom. However, you will soon find that every difference isn't that easy to accept or embrace. Inevitably, you will encounter one or more of the following people.

The Neat Freak

This is the person who knows that everything has a proper place, and should be kept there at all times, including everything on your side of the room. The slightest amount of disorganization or perceived filth is enough to send him/her into a cleaning frenzy. Cleaning supplies and hand sanitizer are constant staples on this person's side of the room.

The Slob

Beware of this person. The "proper place" for anything is wherever it was thrown, dropped, or left. "Clean your room" was rarely enforced at home, if ever. On his/her side of the room, the bed is seldom made, and why would it be, if it will be slept in again? You will usually find clothes, accessories, papers, and possibly food all over the place. Don't be surprised if strange smells emerge from this side of the room. Just hope that nothing that crawls does!

The Social Butterfly

If there's a party, event, concert, or anything else fun, this person definitely knows about it first. He/she may be very well adjusted to the social aspect of college life. However, mastering the academic side is more difficult. You will definitely have a great time with this student. Be careful to remember your priorities and the word "moderation."

The Social Misfit

This is the person who would much rather be alone than deal with you or anyone else, for that matter. There may be exceptions to this rule, such as friends from home, family, and teammates. For the most part, this person is not interested in making friends, and that's all there is to it. He/she doesn't have much to say to you, and may prefer you two not even share a room.

The Brat

This person has never heard the word "no." He/she is used to a life of privilege, so adjusting to college life can present a challenge at times. You may find this person won't or doesn't know how to do certain things, like wash clothes for example. In the event of any crisis (e.g. running out of change to wash clothes), this person has mom, dad, or someone on speed dial to address it.

The Hater

This person is secretly (or explicitly) jealous of you (and usually others) for whatever reason. You may find everything between the two of you becomes a competition, since he/she is always trying to "one-up" you.

The Thief

This person may be known by his/her other name, "The Hater." For some reason, the fact that you left it out (or have it at all) gives him/her the right to take it. It may start with small things, like books, toiletries, etc., and progress to larger items like jewelry, cash, and clothing. If you suspect this is occurring, don't try to handle this yourself. Contact your parents and residence advisor immediately.

The Innkeeper

This person loves overnight guests. Whether it's family, friends, or a significant other, "The Innkeeper" is constantly housing someone for one or more nights. This can present a number of problems when there is always a third (or more) roommate present.

Do you see why it's better to room with someone you know, if at all possible? Each one of the people described above presents their own challenges. The key is to identify them early, determine your level of interaction, and resolve any issues that arise as soon as possible. For example, if your roommate is "The

Slob," there may need to be some early conversations about maintaining your room in a manner that respects everyone's personal space and upholds a decent level of cleanliness. Try establishing a clean-up day each week, and limiting the type and amount of trash stored in your room to avoid problems.

Roommates Don't Always Get Along

You've never met before, and now you're forced to live with one or more people for nine months. What if you don't get along? Everyone isn't fortunate enough to know his or her roommate or get along after meeting. So what do you do, in the event you *don't* get along with your roommate? There are a few ways to address this:

1. *Find out if you really don't get along or simply don't know each other.* This can be difficult if one or both of you aren't that sociable. Invite him/her to hang out with you in the dining hall or start a casual conversation when the two of you are alone in your room.

2. *Find out what the root of the problem is.* This will only happen when you first open the lines of communication. You may find that your roommate doesn't like your friends hanging out in the room so much, or that you keep the music and television too loud while he/she is studying. You may also find that your roommate is shy or homesick, and isn't as outgoing as you are. In these cases, things can usually be resolved quickly. However, if it can't, you may have to try more drastic measures.

3. *Speak to the resident advisor.* If things can't be resolved between the two of you peacefully, then it may be best that you part ways. Unfortunately, this happens. The added stress of not getting along with your roommate is unnecessary and can be overwhelming, especially when you have to live with this person for nine months. Sometimes it's better to just agree to disagree and move on. If your resident advisor can't resolve things, then you may need to speak to someone in your university's residence life office.

4. *Keep documentation.* Make sure you have documented all issues, how you tried to resolve them, and what the current status is. This allows all parties to accurately review the history between the two of you. Also be sure your parents are aware of the issue. While this is your responsibility to address, it is always a good idea to keep your parents aware of any issues that you encounter while in school.

While it's important to meet new people, you have to be comfortable in your living environment. Do not hesitate to address any issues as they arise. So much of your time will be spent in your room. Remember, this is your home away from home

You Don't Know the Friends and Family

So you don't have the previously described problem. You and your roommate get along great. Then his/her childhood friend visits and suddenly, your watch is missing or your side of the room becomes his/her personal hangout.

How do you handle the friends and family, who will inevitably visit? They may be there for a few minutes or a few days, but one thing is certain: you can't wait for them to leave! Don't think that this only applies to non-students. The same goes for that hall mate who loves to hang out in your room. Once the two of you are settled, you and your roommate should discuss a few things:

1. *Agree to visiting hours.* You may prefer to study between 12pm and 2pm, for example, so having visitors during this time is a major distraction. Coming to some understanding early about these things will eliminate anyone feeling like their personal space and time is invaded.

2. *Give advance notice about visitors.* Your roommate may not be that happy that your parents stopped by unexpectedly and he/she is still in pajamas! A little courtesy goes a long way.

3. *Discuss the use of personal space.* For example, if you prefer that your roommate's guests not sit on your bed, use your computer, etc. then discuss that. To make the conversation comfortable for both of you, try starting it with "I wanted to let you know that if I have any guests, I will be sure they respect your space and privacy and do not use any of your belongings." This will show that you are taking the initial steps of respecting personal space. Hopefully your roommate will do the same.

4. *Secure all valuables.* Regardless of whether there are visitors or not, this should be a common practice. You should have some means of securely storing items in your room (e.g. closet, drawer, etc.). If you can't, then consider purchasing a chest or foot locker that can be stored under your bed or in the closet. Remember, most residence halls are not responsible for any damage to or theft of personal belongings.

Flip-Flops and Shower Caddies Are Your Friends

Call me high maintenance, but community bathrooms and showers are cruel and unusual punishment. Unfortunately, you are not the only person using these facilities, which means you never know what is waiting for you upon entry. My first night on campus, I was horrified to see a hall mate walk into the bathroom barefoot! The horror!

Having a pair of flip-flops for the shower and around the dorm provides a level of protection (as well as sanitation). A shower caddy can store all of your toiletries (e.g. soap, toothbrush, toothpaste, shampoo, etc.) so you don't have to worry about carrying a dozen items into the bathroom every time you get dressed.

Something Won't Work in Your Dorm or Room

My first day in the freshman dorm was a great time to realize there was no central air conditioning. Later, when fall came and it was a little chilly in the mornings, we were informed that the heat was controlled centrally from an off-campus location. When it did finally turn on, there was no temperature control! But wait, there's more. There was also the time that one of the toilets overflowed in the bathroom (which made me all the more grateful for my flip-flops and shower caddy). Seriously, how much more could you expect an 18-year-old only child to take?

I learned two important things that year. First, something will inevitably not work. This is usually when you *really* need it! Second, you are going to have to learn to adjust. Unfortunately, you can't control these things, and you will have to adapt accordingly. We learned to open our window just enough to cool the room off, when the mono-temperature heat was too unbearable. And remember, while these may seem like drastic events in the moment, these hiccups are but a few of the cherished memories that you will laugh about after you graduate. Seriously, I laughed as I wrote this.

You Won't Like the Cafeteria Food

Get over it. At some point, you are *not* going to enjoy the on-campus dining experience. The hours are too early or limited, the food isn't good, the selection is too limited, or you have a restricted diet. The list goes on. If you are fortunate enough to attend a university that has more than one option for dining, then you may be able to circumvent this. However, be mindful of how your meal plan is structured, and what this will cost you.

If there is only one dining hall available, verify your options for storing food in your room. Some dorms prohibit personal refrigerators or microwaves. If this is the case, you may have to share the community kitchen. This means any food or drinks that must be refrigerated may or may not be there when you want them. You should still be able to store non-perishables (e.g. crackers, chips, cookies, and drinks) in your room.

Alternately, if you have a car or other means for traveling off campus, you can always choose to dine at a local restaurant. Just know that these meals can be costly. If you have a limited amount of money, then it is best to adapt to the on-campus options, especially since you already paid for them. I learned to like *something* in the cafeteria daily. Sure, I may have eaten more hot dogs than I cared to, but it was part of my meal plan, and I always had fish Fridays to look forward to (followed by fish Saturday and Sunday)!

Crimes Happen on Campus

Unfortunately, there are a number of crimes that can happen on a college campus. It's important that you are aware of these, notice the signs of any, and are prepared to act, should you or anyone you know find yourselves in these situations. Too often, we hear news reports of a missing college student, assaults, or campus shootings. While this is not the case on every campus, it's important that you understand that it *could* happen if you are not careful. Being on a college campus does not protect you from becoming a victim of crime. You must take precautionary steps, such as those outlined below, to ensure that you protect yourself at all times:

1. *Keep the number to campus security.* This is the most important number you should have. Keep it stored in your cell phone as well as your room.

2. *Keep a landline phone in your room.* In the age of cell phones, many students feel they don't need a landline phone. For a number of emergency purposes, keep an inexpensive one anyway.

3. *Locate campus blue lights, and make sure you know how to use them.* These lights are placed around campus, in the event that you encounter an emergency and need to quickly notify security.

4. *There is safety in numbers.* If walking at night, through enclosed/wooded areas, or to off-campus locations, have others with you. My friends and I were teased in college for constantly traveling in large groups. However, we were inadvertently protecting each other from a number of potential incidents.

5. *Keep your room locked at ALL times.* You are just running to the bathroom, and you don't feel like taking your keys with you, right? It's just down the hall and will only take two minutes. *WRONG.* It only takes a few

seconds for someone to break into your room, especially if unlocked. Even if you go next door, *ALWAYS* lock your door. This should be a common practice for both you and your roommate. When you are in the room, keep it locked to prevent uninvited guests from easily entering.

6. *Be aware of your surroundings.* Distractions of any kind make you less aware of what is going on around you. Just about every college student has a cell phone, MP3 player, or both. I constantly pass students walking on campus wearing headphones or chatting on their phone, totally oblivious to their surroundings. Think about how hard it is to hear someone approaching with headphones on. How aware of your surroundings are you? These can become dangerous distractions. If you are alone, especially at night, *DO NOT* use these until you are in a secure building, car, etc. However, *DO* keep your phone easily accessible, should you need it for emergency purposes. In addition, do not get in and out of vehicles (day or night) while using these, as you are again unaware of your surroundings. Remember, anyone watching you will notice this. Remain aware of streets, locations, landmarks, and people that you pass while traveling.

7. *Request a campus escort, if necessary.* You may have a class that ends at night, or you need to go to the library late. Find a group of students who can travel with you to these locations. If you can't find anyone, contact campus security to request an escort. These are individuals who safely chaperone students to/from various on-campus locations. If your campus is open (meaning accessible to the public), then it's even more important to practice these safety precautions.

8. *Tell at least two people where you are going and who you will be with.* This is something I practice even now. Always let others know where you are going, when you expect to return, and who you will be with. If there are

any changes, notify these people while in the presence of your company. This makes everyone aware that others know of your whereabouts and who you are with. Include *all* contact information (e.g. phone numbers, addresses, email, car make and model, description, etc.). While this may seem extreme, this was a good practice that my girlfriends and I always followed, especially when meeting new people and going on dates. Remember, you are in a new environment and will be meeting new people daily. Be safe and always remain in public areas with people you don't know.

Know the Facts about Off-Campus Housing

You may have lived on campus your freshman year and now you want to get an apartment. You couldn't stand the rules, the shared bathrooms, and the roommate. There is a lot to consider before you move:

1. *An apartment may not be cheaper.* Many students think this will automatically be the case. You are no longer paying for room and board, so your balance owed to the university does decrease. However, depending on the cost of living in the nearby area, you may spend more on rent *plus* utilities, food, etc. You also want to be somewhere safe, so that will influence the location and costs.

2. *You will have monthly bills.* This was something I DEFINITELY did not want. With an apartment comes monthly bills that must be paid. If your parents aren't going to help you, then you need a job to sustain yourself.

3. *You are now responsible for everything.* In addition to bills, you have to eat, clean, and maintain your household. Are you ready for that responsibility?

4. *You are not surrounded by students or a college campus.* Your new complex or building will include people of all ages and backgrounds. This is important to understand

when it relates to your personal safety. You may be more susceptible to random crimes, because there is no campus police or security monitoring the grounds.

5. *It's going to take longer to get to/from class.* Living off campus means that you must now identify a means of transportation to/from campus. In addition, you can't simply walk back to your room between classes.

6. *You are going to miss out on some of the fun of living on campus.* I remember sitting on the block or outside the dorms on a nice day, people watching and talking to friends. These random moments will be missed when you no longer live on campus.

It should be noted that there are some students who must live off campus. For example, if you have a family, there may not be any on-campus housing available that would meet your needs. Your campus experience will, of course, be different than a student who is simply choosing not to live on campus.

Second, if your university does not guarantee housing for upperclassmen, then you may not have a choice either. I strongly suggest that you first try to qualify for on-campus housing. If you must find off-campus housing, then find something that is in a safe area, affordable, and an easy commute to/from campus. You may find that having a roommate (preferably another student) will help minimize your individual expenses, and increase the combined amount you can afford to pay in rent.

Many universities have suite-like dorms that are similar to on-campus apartments. Students have individual rooms, but share a bathroom and common area with one or two other students. These provide some of the perks of off-campus living, with the convenience of remaining on campus.

Step Two

Have a Resume and Professional Attire

If you read *Prepped for Success*, then you know the importance of your resume when submitting college admissions applications. Now that you are a college student, your resume becomes even more important. This document will be a continuous work in progress that you will use for the rest of your professional career.

Your resume is used by potential employers to identify if you are a good candidate for any job opportunities, including internships, co-ops, research experiences, and post-graduation employment. You will learn more about these in chapter 8. You will also use your resume when attending career fairs and applying for scholarships, fellowships, and graduate school.

Your resume is similar to a brag sheet. It should contain enough information to convince a potential employer that you are the best candidate for the position. If you've never created a resume before, then use the sample resume as a template. You can find other templates online.

The *Objectives* section of your resume should describe (in no more than two sentences) what your career goal is. Be very brief and detailed. In addition, tailor this statement to the position you are applying for.

The *Skills* section of your resume should list the skills that help you qualify for the position. Be sure to include skills that you consider yourself to be at least proficient in. If you are learning new skills, then note your level of experience accordingly.

John Student
John.student@myemail.com
111 My Street
City, State
(123)456-7890

Objective	To obtain experience in the field of any field as a successful any job.
Skills	-Highlight any skills that you consider yourself to be proficient in that may be helpful in the position you are applying for (computer software, presentation, writing, teamwork, etc.)
Work Experience	Year Company Name, Title, Department
List all responsibilities the position included, such as greeting customers, data entry, customer service, etc.
Education	Your University, City, State
Expected Graduation Date: Month, Year
GPA: 4.0/4.0
Relevant Courses	-Biology I/II -Economic Principles
-Marketing   -Calculus I/II
Activities	-Volunteer Work -Organizations
-Any Other Relevant Extracurricular Activities You Participated In
Honors	-Academic Awards -Extracurricular Awards
-Honor Societies, Other Awards Received
References	Available Upon Request

The *Work Experience* section will be updated every year for the rest of your academic and professional career. List no more than the three most recent positions that are relevant to the position you are applying to. Since you are a college student, it's ok to list your three most recent positions, even if they aren't relevant to your career interests. If you held any leadership positions or responsibility, then be sure to include this information. For each position, you should paraphrase your experience in no more than three sentences. It's ok if these are incomplete sentences, as long as they clearly identify your responsibilities in this position. Each year, you should update this section to replace the least recent position with the one you just recently completed.

Since you are a college student, your *Education* section includes your high school and college information. If you are at least a sophomore, then most employers will focus heavily on your college information. Be sure to include your cumulative GPA. Many students think that including the GPA within their major will help them, especially if it's higher than their cumulative GPA. This isn't necessarily true. Employers will still request your transcript. Any difference will be questioned. If you've had any hiccups in the semester, then be prepared to explain this. It's better to be upfront and honest.

In the *Relevant Courses* section, list the courses you've completed that have best prepared you for this position. These will usually be courses in your major.

In the *Activities* section, list the most recent activities that you've participated in. These can include on and off campus activities, as well as those that you participated in during high school. If you held any leadership positions, be sure to note these. This section helps to highlight how diverse you are.

In the *Honors* section, make sure that you list all awards and honors received, including honors society, honor roll, scholarships, and more. Remember, this is similar to your brag sheet. You must sell yourself.

Most employers will want references. These are similar to recommendations you requested for your college admissions application. Instead of identifying individuals who will provide these (because they can change each semester and year), simply list that they will be provided upon request.

It is important to remember the following when creating your resume:

1. *It should be NO LONGER THAN ONE PAGE.* As a college student, you should not have a resume longer than one page. Once you have created your document, adjust the font type, font size, spacing, and/or page margins, if necessary.

2. *Use only basic, clear fonts.* These are fonts like Times New Roman, Arial, etc. In addition, font sizes should be no smaller than 9 or 10pt. Do not use colored paper.

3. *Use a professional email address.* Free ones are available from a number of websites (e.g. Yahoo, Hotmail, and Gmail). A good choice is always some combination of first, middle, and last names and/or initials. If these are taken, using a year of significance is also acceptable, such as john.brown@email.com, jbrown00@email.com, etc. *NEVER* use an email address that is not considered professional, such as flygirl12@email.com.

4. *Update your resume at the end of each semester/year.* Include new information, such as courses, jobs, awards, and activities. As new items are added, some items can be removed. The most current and applicable information is what will remain on the resume. This will ensure you always have an accurate and detailed account of your activities and accomplishments.

5. *Document everything, but be concise.* Be sure to list any relevant courses, activities, sports, volunteer work, awards, and honors that will help sell you. If a bulleted item is longer than one column, place it last on the list, such as in the "Honors" section of the sample resume.

Attire

In addition to your resume, you should always have at least one professional outfit. I understand that, as college students, you may not have a lot of money. However, you can find an inexpensive outfit and shoes to serve this purpose. You never know when you will need it for interviews, meetings, special events, and more. Gentlemen, be sure to have a suit, tie, and dress shoes. Ladies, have a dress or suit and dress shoes. This is completely different from any outfit and shoes that you would wear to the club, FYI.

Depending on your intended major, you will need this attire more often than you think. Many business departments require students to dress in professional attire at least once a week. You can find these outfits at a number of stores in the mall that don't require spending a lot of money. Whatever you purchase, make sure it is of a decent quality that you will be able to wear it more than once. If you aren't sure where to find these, speak to classmates, professors, and staff members on campus to find shops in your local area.

Step Three

Know, Understand, and Remember Registration, Advising, and Graduation Requirements

As a professor, I often find myself reminding students of the real reason they are in college: to successfully pursue and complete a degree. While this seems pretty obvious, even the best student can sometimes forget this. Between homecoming, hanging out on the yard, and athletic and social events, you can easily forget that your studies are your main priority. How often and to what extent you forget this can result in minor to significant issues along your academic journey.

The next three chapters are designed to provide you with strategies that will help you navigate through or around any academic challenges you encounter. I chose to present this information across three chapters for a few reasons. First, successfully completing your education requires more than just passing courses. You must know what courses to complete, when to complete them, and how many to complete per semester to maintain your financial aid, good academic standing, and more.

Second, many students do not fully utilize the resources available to help them. Next, many students do not have good time management or study skills. Finally, many students (and parents) do not understand the academic code of conduct, the implications of violating it, and the rights of parents to question or obtain academic records.

This chapter focuses on your major, advisor, plan of study, and the registration process. Chapter 4 focuses on strategies for successfully completing courses. Finally, chapter 5 focuses on developing good time management and study skills, as well as maintaining good academic standing.

Regardless of your classification, you will find something of value in each chapter. Each semester, I encounter students who fall victim to a variety of academic mistakes that could have been easily avoided if they were sufficiently prepared, made better choices, or heeded the advice of those attempting to intervene. The consequences of these mistakes range from a lower GPA to losing scholarships or, worse, being suspended from the university. To avoid any of these consequences, you should not only read, but implement the following suggestions.

Choose the "Right" Major

In *Prepped for Success*, you learned how to identify the best major for you, when submitting college applications. Many colleges and universities require incoming freshmen to declare a major. I don't like this requirement for a number of reasons. At 18 years old, I thought I wanted to major in marketing. I had some glamorous idea of what a person in marketing does. What that was exactly, I couldn't tell you. All I knew was that it sounded great and involved business. While I liked working with computers (and did well in my high-school programming courses), I thought I would minor in computer science as more of a "plan B."

My freshman year, I was encouraged by my Introduction to Programming professor to consider computer science as my major and minor in marketing. His argument was "you will have more options in computer science and learn how integral it will be to everything in the near future." That was the spring of 1997. How right he was! I ultimately declared computer science as my major and forgot all about a minor.

My story is similar to many high-school graduates, incoming freshman, and (in some cases) undecided upperclassmen. Many of you really don't have a clear understanding of the requirements within a major, career options available, and course requirements as an incoming freshman. So how can you *know* that you want to major in mass communications when you don't know the difference between this major and public relations, for example?

Second, many students declare majors for the wrong reasons. Your parents want you to become a lawyer, so you decide to major in criminal justice. Your true passion though is early childhood education. Similarly, you declare a major in computer science, because you've seen how much money can be made through the development of websites like Facebook, YouTube, etc. The only problem is that you're not that strong in math, and prefer to take as little as possible. In either of these cases, the major that you declared may not be the best one for you.

There are a number of consequences that can result from not choosing a major wisely. Suppose you complete a number of freshman-level courses in your major. If you don't perform well, then your GPA can be significantly affected, regardless of whether you change majors later or not. Second, you may end up wasting credit hours in courses that won't count towards graduation, should you decide to change your major. This may result in spending extra semesters in school, which also means additional expenses. For these reasons, it's important that you make the best decision regarding your major as early as possible. This means making the best decision for *you*. Remember, you are the person who must ultimately find and build a career in this area. This should be your decision, with the trusted support of family, friends, and other individuals who are genuinely vested in your academic and professional success. To help you make that decision, consider the following:

1. *Be realistic.* First, be honest with yourself and your family. Identify your career interests, the majors that lead to this career, courses required in these majors, and your academic strengths and challenges. This will help you identify the expectations of the major and career, and your level of preparation to pursue them. Just because you aren't strong in a subject does not necessarily mean you shouldn't consider that major. However, it *does* mean that you must be realistic. Pursuing this major will

probably mean extra studying, preliminary courses, and tutoring. This requires a level of commitment on your part.

2. *Meet with the department chair.* This person is one of the most helpful resources when trying to determine if the major is the best fit. Discuss your interests, academic background, current progress, and what your next steps should be. If it is determined that you need to make improvements in certain areas, he/she can help you identify how to accomplish this. Be sure that, when meeting with the department chair, you have all necessary documents with you, including your high-school transcript (incoming freshmen), or your current transcript and plan of study (returning or transfer students). You will learn more about the plan of study later in this chapter.

3. *Review additional material on majors and careers.* This is where speaking with the department chair will be very beneficial. You may think of the most obvious courses and careers, but the department chair can help you identify additional opportunities. Many majors are now so interdisciplinary that you can find a career in just about any field. You can even create your own! I have a friend who pursued her B.S., M.S., and Ph.D. in chemistry, so that she could create her own line of hair care products!

So what if you find yourself in a major that you no longer want to pursue? How do you address this issue with as little collateral damage as possible? First, consult your advisor. He/she can guide you through this process and provide direction as needed.

Next, speak to the chair of the new department you intend to transfer into. He/she can provide information on entry requirements, if course credits from the previous major will be accepted, the plan of study, and your expected timeline for completion of the degree.

Finally, be extremely cautious in making this decision. It is important that it is well-planned, after consulting with your department chairs, advisor, and parents. Remember, you are the person pursuing this degree and ultimately career. You will be the one most affected by the choices you make.

Refer to Your Plan of Study Frequently

Every department has a proposed course sequence that identifies the courses you should complete each semester from freshman through senior year. This is your plan of study, a multi-year outline of the courses required to complete your degree, the sequence in which they should be completed, and the total number of credit hours required to graduate. You can usually obtain this document from the department (in person or online) or the university handbook.

During freshman orientation, my university president, Dr. Dorothy Yancy, advised each of us to keep our handbook as if it was our most prized possession. According to her, it would ultimately help those of us who heeded her advice, and hinder those who didn't. How right she was!

At the end of each semester, update your plan of study to include the grades received from each course. Next, identify your proposed schedule for the upcoming semester, based on the remaining requirements. I remember classmates who were surprised to learn, a few days before graduation, that they were missing one course or didn't pass another and couldn't graduate. If they were accurately updating their plan of study each year, they would have easily avoided this unfortunate and embarrassing situation.

As a professor, I witness this each spring. Student X waits until his senior year to take my course. He earned a 'D' in my course, when the minimum grade requirement was a 'C,' and now cannot graduate. Even worse are situations where students must retake a course that is only offered once per academic year. Keeping this updated plan of study will ensure you avoid such obstacles. This is where your advisor and department chair will be of great benefit.

Work Closely With Your Advisor

Along with the department chair, your academic advisor is one of the most important people you will meet in college. He/she is a faculty member (usually in your department) who is assigned to help you follow your plan of study, complete your courses in a timely manner, and remain on track academically to graduate. Your advisor may change over time. However, his/her purpose does not. If you are an incoming student, you will typically be assigned an advisor. The two of you should meet to discuss your interests, academic performance in high school, and suggestions for successfully beginning and completing your freshman year.

You should meet with your advisor at *least* three times per semester: the beginning of the semester, after midterm exams, and before final exams. Each meeting, you should discuss your progress in each course. Around midterms, you should also discuss feedback from your professors, and determine if you should remain in the courses or drop some. Before final exams, you should discuss your expected grades, proposed schedule for the upcoming semester, and ensure that you are on track to graduate, according to your plan of study. Your advisor can also help you navigate through any issues you encounter, including academic, personal, and more.

My advisor at JCSU was Dr. Magdy Attia. He was also the department chair, and became a sounding board for me to discuss my interests, courses, academic progress, and more. Dr. Attia became one of my biggest advocates. Because I made myself known to him and performed well in my courses, he also began to recommend me for scholarships, internships, and other special events. To this day, we still have a great relationship. I've tried to provide this same support to my undergraduates, especially since this support is the only reason you are reading this book.

So what if you don't like or are uncomfortable with your advisor? This can and does happen. In the event that it does, you have a few options. First, talk to your department chair about finding a new one. Students are usually assigned advisors based on classification, last name, etc. There may be other faculty members that you are more comfortable working with. If you have identified someone, ask if he/she would serve as your advisor. If agreed upon, notify the department chair to ensure that any documentation is properly completed. I've had several students request I serve as their advisor and others who preferred to work with someone else. It's a matter of preference. We don't take it personal.

It's important to understand that your advisor's purpose is to help you successfully complete your degree. It's your responsibility to be honest and upfront at *all* times regarding your grades, upcoming course schedule, and any issues that arise. We can offer strategies on how to best address any of these. However, to do so, we have to be fully aware of your situation. In addition, we can't make you follow our directions. It would be in your best interest to follow it though, given that we have experience with this process. If you choose not to follow our instructions, then you are responsible for the consequences, good or bad. One of the keys to your success at the university is being *honest and proactive*. At the end of the day, it is *your* academic success that is at stake.

Understand How to Add, Drop, and Audit Courses

Your advisor and plan of study are both very important as you add, drop, and audit courses. Registration can be frustrating and unsuccessful, especially if you are not well prepared. In addition, auditing and dropping courses without a plan can be very costly in terms of time and money. Auditing courses means that you are registered for the course, but will not receive credit for completion. Following the steps below will help guarantee you make well-planned decisions when completing this process:

1. *Be aware of each registration period.* These typically occur multiple times per semester. For the fall, registration occurs during the preceding spring semester (returning students), summer break (new and returning students), and beginning of the fall semester (all

students). For the spring, these periods include the preceding fall semester (returning students), winter break (new and returning students), and beginning of the spring semester (all students). You can find this information on the university calendar or by contacting your advisor.

2. *Register as early as possible.* This is why it is important to keep your plan of study updated. If you know when the registration periods occur, you can quickly develop a proposed schedule for the upcoming semester. Depending on the course, department, or university, courses can fill up quickly. University-wide requirements, freshman-level, and general courses, such as science, math, and English may have high student enrollment. As a result, they may reach maximum capacity quickly. One mistake I see a number of students make is not registering for courses because the only available section is early in the morning. These decisions can cost you a semester or more in terms of your expected graduation, especially if the course is a prerequisite for other courses. Finally, if you register for a course during the first few weeks of class, *you* are responsible for obtaining and completing any missed material, including lecture notes and assignments.

3. *Register for at least 15 credit hours per semester.* Full-time status is 12 credit hours. By enrolling in a minimum of 15, you have provided yourself some wiggle room to drop one course, if necessary. Again, refer to your plan of study to identify how many credit hours you should complete per semester in order to graduate on time.

4. *Only audit or drop a course you can afford to retake.* This is why it's important to register for a minimum of 15 credit hours. If you aren't performing well in a class, you can drop or audit it, so that it doesn't affect your GPA. This means you can retake the course another semester. However, be sure that this decision will not affect your target graduation date. For example, if a

course is offered once per year, but is a prerequisite for other courses, you may be delayed in your graduation.

5. *Consult your advisor before modifying your course schedule.* This ensures that the two of you are on the same accord. In addition, your advisor can determine if the modifications will affect future courses or your expected graduation.

Your advisor, plan of study, and registration savvy are critical to your academic success. I recently encountered a second-semester freshman who was failing my course miserably. I couldn't understand why, after failing the midterm exam, he didn't drop the course before the deadline. The student finally came to my office hours two weeks before the last day of class to discuss his performance. When asked why he didn't withdraw, he stated that he only registered for 14 credit hours that semester and would only have 11 if he dropped the course. He would then be below full-time status and lose his scholarship. The twisted irony of this story was that his performance in my course, as well as two more, already caused him to lose his scholarship, because his GPA dropped below a 3.0.

When asked why he had not enrolled in more credit hours at the beginning of the semester, the student stated he wasn't aware he could drop courses. According to him, his advisor never discussed that. Only a second-semester freshman, the student had now lost his academic scholarship (which he could not reapply for), and would have to obtain student loans to cover the cost of attendance for the next academic year.

Unfortunately, this story is common to many students. This is why it's important to have an advisor who you are comfortable with, ask questions, and be as proactive as possible each semester. I'll never know what his advisor provided in terms of information or if the student simply didn't heed his/her advice. However, one thing is certain: the student ultimately suffered academically and financially.

Step Four
Your Classes Are Your Priority

As discussed in chapter 3, the reason you are in college is to complete your degree. To do so, you must successfully complete your courses. Each year, I warn students on the first day of class to make choices that will have a positive impact on their academic, personal, and professional development. Unfortunately, there are always a few who fail to heed this warning and suffer the consequences, such as failing one or more courses. If this doesn't seem like a serious offense to you, then think again. Failing a course can result in a lost scholarship, delayed graduation, academic suspension, or expulsion. To avoid this situation, take heed to the information in this chapter.

Review the Syllabus Frequently

On the first day of class, you should receive a course syllabus from your professor. This document contains a *wealth* of information that many students overlook and often discard. It usually includes the course description, prerequisites, required text, topics covered, and grading criteria. Pay close attention to grading. If you have any questions regarding the syllabus or class, then ask your professor. It's important to remember the syllabus is a contract. Keep this document each semester for your academic records. This holds you as well as your professors accountable.

You Are Responsible for Missed Material

This is important to reiterate. You can miss a lot of information within the first few weeks of the semester. Register as early as possible for courses, and contact your professor to obtain any missed info if you register after the course begins.

You Must Purchase the Book (And Read It)

I try to have lecture notes available to students prior to beginning each chapter's in-class discussion. This eliminates the risk of students missing part of the lecture because they are more focused on copying the notes than listening to me and understanding the material. I'll never forget one student who approached me after class and asked, "are you going to provide lecture notes for each chapter?" I replied, "yes, but the notes don't cover all of the reading material. You still need to read." He paused, slightly confused by my response. "So, when do we need to get the book?" I should note that this would have been a more appropriate question, were it the first week of class. However, since we were ending the third week, I simply responded "three weeks ago" and walked away with a look of disgust.

Here is a word of advice that all students reading this should understand. The book is assigned for a reason. Lecture notes, just like class lectures, are designed to *supplement* the reading material, not replace it. If you do not have the book or simply choose not to read it, then you have already put yourself at a disadvantage in the course. The further behind you get, the more difficult it will be to not only catch up, but also pass. It is much easier to read ahead of or with the class. As you read, make note of any topics that are unclear. Be prepared to ask questions in class, should you need further explanation. Remember, majority of your academic success depends upon you being proactive.

I completely understand that textbooks are expensive. Depending on your financial status, purchasing a new textbook for each course can be a strain. There are a number of options for purchasing used textbooks from your campus bookstore, other students, and online. Check your campus library to see if any copies are available. Finally, ask a classmate if he/she would share the cost of purchasing the textbook. Whatever your method, you are still responsible for the material covered in class.

Be on Time for Class and Pay Attention

Reading the book will give you the fundamental background. However, class lectures are designed to further explain concepts. In order to fully maximize your learning, you must regularly attend class. In my courses, pop quizzes are randomly given during the first 10 minutes of class. Despite knowing this, many students are repeatedly late. The purpose of these quizzes is not only to ensure students are reading and studying outside of class, but also to illustrate the importance of punctuality. When arriving to interviews, meetings, or jobs, you must be punctual. Many employers will not accept excuses that you overslept or were stuck in traffic. Being late may cost you an important project, job, or in this case grade.

I don't think paying attention in class requires much explanation. However, this still seems to be an issue for some students. With so much technology at your fingertips, it's easy to become distracted by your laptop, MP3 player, or cell phone. If being used for class purposes, then these are great learning tools. However, if you are listening to your favorite song or texting a friend, you can easily miss important material. The same applies for classmates. If you are talking during class discussions, then you are missing important information that may not be discussed in the lecture notes or textbook. In addition, please stay awake! If we have to stay awake to teach then you need to stay awake to learn.

If your professor is generous enough to provide lecture notes prior to class, *print and review them!* I'm amazed how many students don't print the lecture notes, but still attempt to copy them in class. Note any questions that you have and be prepared to ask them during the next class lecture. Some of my students record the lectures using a recorder or cell phone. They can review the audio at their convenience, and are able to focus more on the discussion.

Do Your Homework

Contrary to popular opinion, we do not assign homework to punish you or monopolize your time. It is designed to help you understand the concepts presented in the reading and class. I have never met a student who passed my course without completing the homework. This is typically because the homework helps prepare students for all other graded assignments, including projects, quizzes, and exams. In some courses, your professor may not grade assignments. These are designed to be practice problems for you to complete throughout the semester. It is even more important that you complete these in preparation for graded exams, projects, etc.

My homework policy requires all assignments to be submitted online. Students are warned that if the assignment is received one minute past the deadline, it is not accepted and their grade is a 0. Some would find this too strict. However, if you are working in your career, you have deadlines that you are expected to meet. If you miss these, then you can potentially lose money and your job. As a child, my father would always tell me "you play how you practice." The habits you form or continue to practice in college are the same ones that you will have when you enter your career, good or bad. It's important that these work to your advantage as much as possible.

Your Professors Should Know Your Name

Depending on the size of your university and classes, this may be more difficult to accomplish. However, it *can* and *should* be done. My average class size is about 25 students. Each semester, I tell students on the first day that if I don't know your name (for the right reasons) by the time midterm grades are submitted, then you are not doing a good job of standing out.

It may not seem as apparent why you should want to stand out to your professors, but think about this. As a professor, I constantly receive information about scholarship, internship, and job opportunities. Many of these require recommending a student within a few days or even hours. The students that are usually recommended are those that I remember from class who are on time, have a great work ethic, stay awake, always participate and ask questions, and have good grades (or at least put forth maximum effort). In other words, these are the students who stand out enough for me to easily remember them.

You always want professors to think of you in this respect. Remember how you needed teacher recommendations for your college admissions applications? This required having an established, positive relationship with teachers who could speak favorably of you. You will need this again in college. You never know what opportunities your professors, deans, or presidents have access to. You *always* want to be that student that they immediately think of.

Plagiarism and Cheating is Unacceptable

The World Wide Web has made it easy for students to access information 24 hours a day. However, you *must* understand the difference between gaining more understanding and copying answers. Many universities have strict academic codes of conduct. Plagiarism and cheating can result in failing the course as well as expulsion from the university. Even if you avoid any university punishment, you have seriously handicapped yourself with regards to your academic and professional career. You don't truly understand the material, which can have a number of negative consequences, even when interviewing for jobs where you are expected to know it. Do you really want to risk your academic and professional career for such a stupid act? Remember, if you follow the instructions outlined in this chapter, you won't need to worry about cheating or plagiarizing.

Visit Office Hours and Teacher Assistants (TAs)

Office hours are times that professors make themselves available to answer questions regarding class, lectures, reading material, and assignments. Your course may also have a TA, who is usually a graduate student or undergraduate who previously completed the course. He/she provides extra assistance outside of the professor's office hours, including study sessions and labs.

It's amazing how many students will struggle through a semester and never visit the professor or TA for assistance. Office hours are an excellent opportunity for you to become well known to your professor. It's also a great time for you to get one-on-one assistance with any course material. Be sure that you are prepared for any visit to office hours with the professor or TA. Don't show up without any class material and say "I don't understand anything." We expect that you've attempted something, reached a point that you are stuck, and can articulate this to us.

Track Your Progress

The grading structure for each course should be outlined in the course syllabus. This is why it's important to keep this document. For every graded assignment, quiz, test, or project, you should be able to determine your current grade in the course at any time. This will help you identify areas of improvement and if you should remain in the course or drop it.

DO NOT Ask for Extra Credit

This has to be the most annoying question that you can ask a professor. I warn students each semester to *NOT* ask for any extra credit opportunities. If provided, extra credit is offered to everyone in the class, not to individuals who now want to increase their grade because they are not passing the course. I always ignore these requests. First, extra credit is not designed to be a game-changer. What do I mean by game-changer? Let's assume your current grade in the course is a 65, which corresponds to a D. After receiving extra credit, your grade increases to a 78, which is a C+.

This significant increase would be another disadvantage to you. By your own merits, you did not earn this grade or pass the course. However, with extra credit you pass and continue your studies with less knowledge than students in your discipline are expected to have. Second, why should extra credit be provided, if you didn't do the work to receive regular credit throughout the academic year? I'm amazed, each semester, when students who didn't complete homework assignments, were frequently late to class (if they came at all), or slept through class ask me to *please* allow them to complete extra credit, because they need to pass the course to maintain their scholarships, GPA, etc. These are things you should be mindful of as you are completing the course. Do the work throughout the semester and you will rarely need extra credit.

Verify AP and Transfer Credits

It is your responsibility to ensure that the university appropriately recognizes AP or transfer credits. I remember taking AP Calculus, English, and US History in high school, all of which I scored high enough on the AP tests to receive college credit. I was so upset when my university admissions office equated my AP Calculus credits to Math 135 and 136, which were College Algebra I and II. After speaking with the admissions officers, I was told I still had to enroll in Calculus I at the university.

A few weeks into the semester, I spoke with the Calculus professor regarding my situation. I requested to take any comprehensive exam that covered all topics in the course, to hopefully place out of it. After passing this exam, my professor agreed to these terms. If you feel like you are not receiving the appropriate credit for a course, then visit your professor or department chair to discuss your situation and any opportunities to resolve it. There may be placement tests that will allow you to waive certain courses. You never know unless you ask. More importantly, make sure that any credits you bring to the university will be best used to your advantage. *Every* credit completed should be one less credit needed to graduate.

Understand Summer School Requirements

Summer school seems like the perfect time to retake courses or take additional ones to get ahead. However, you should fully understand the university's policy regarding summer school, including transferring credit from other universities. Many students go home for the summer and would prefer to take courses at a local university or one where the cost of attendance is cheaper (e.g. community colleges). Be sure that you understand how summer school credits will apply. It is best that you verify this with your department chair prior to the end of the spring semester. This ensures that all of the courses you complete count towards your graduation requirements.

Second, it's important to understand the timeline and pace of summer courses. During the fall and spring semester, you have class only a few days each week. In summer school, you will attend class each day and for longer time periods per day. Understand if summer school is an option that best fits your schedule, needs, and academic expectations. Remember, you must still receive a grade in this course. Are you prepared to complete the reading, assignments, and projects in the abbreviated timeframe to successfully pass the course? Can you balance the course expectations with any other responsibilities you may have during the summer, such as internships? I tried summer school once as a graduate student. That was the worst experience I ever had. The pace, time requirements, and instructor were not conducive to my academic expectations and needs. I managed to finish the course with a B. However, I vowed to never do it again.

Understand the Family Educational Rights and Privacy Act (FERPA)

This law protects the privacy of student education records. Many times, parents want to know how their child is performing in a class, and want to speak directly to the professor. Unless we receive written permission from the student, faculty members are legally prohibited from speaking with parents/guardians regarding student academic records. Of course, many parents become highly frustrated when they hear this. They are paying tuition and taking care of the student, so why should they require permission to find out how their child is performing? One of the simplest ways to avoid this issue is to speak to the university's student services office in advance about the FERPA, discuss it with your parents, and submit the necessary documentation prior to the beginning of the semester.

Do not use the FERPA as a means to deceive your parents on your academic progress. I have encountered students who misinform their parents about grades and sometimes enrollment at the university. This always ends badly. There is always information that students have conveniently neglected to inform their parents of, including the fact that they are not graduating, failed courses, or were suspended. Avoid any drama. Remember, honesty is the best policy.

Do Not Cram for Tests

This can be one of the most exhausting, frustrating, and unsuccessful strategies to attempt. If you follow the strategies outlined in this chapter, including reading with or ahead of the lecture, asking questions both in and out of the classroom, utilizing office hours, etc., then you should have no need to cram before any exam. The information you have been retaining over the course of the semester will give you a solid foundation.

Step Five

Time Management and Study Skills Are Your Best Friends

By now, you probably realize that college life entails a lot more than just attending classes. There are campus events to attend, organizations to join, and more. You can easily fill your calendar from now until the end of the school year! As a college student, I did everything I could possibly imagine: played basketball for three years, joined a sorority, partied, and attended events at other universities. I truly did everything I wanted to do, and maintained a 4.0 GPA while doing it!

How did I manage to do all of these things? It was simple: good time management and study skills. I also followed the principles outlined in chapters 3 and 4, such as keeping my plan of study, establishing great relationships with my advisor and professors, and tracking my performance in each class throughout each semester.

Many of the things outlined in this chapter (as well as the previous two) are things that I learned as a college student. As a high-school student, my parents always made me complete my homework and then review it with them. However, my parents were no longer on campus with me to make sure I studied. In addition, college is much different than high school, as you've already learned or read throughout this book. Some things that helped me succeed in high school would not suffice in college.

One of the biggest mistakes students make is not developing and implementing good time management and study skills. This *must* be one of the first things you do. Remember, every grade you receive from your freshman through senior year is used to calculate your GPA. Surprisingly, developing good time management and study skills is not as difficult as you think.

Nothing in this chapter is newly discovered information. It is what worked for me, as well as countless other college students before and after me. However, too many students undervalue its importance until it's too late.

Get Organized

I learned that when my environment is cluttered, my mind is as well. Before I can accomplish any work, I have to clean. Whether it's my house or office, I can't work in a chaotic environment. If your living space is cluttered, make sure you clean it.

Second, get a folder or notebook for each course. The first document in each folder should be the course syllabus. Keep all graded assignments, lecture notes, etc. organized. Finally, if you are like me, and tend to write quickly (and not so legibly) during class, rewrite any notes, so that they are more legible when you study.

Getting organized can be a life-saver when you are balancing multiple courses per semester, especially when each course includes assignments, projects, and more. It will also assist you when meeting with the professor and TA during office hours. Remember, you should be prepared for any office hours or study session you attend. This means bringing any reading and graded material.

Manage Your Time Wisely

The first major difference between high school and college is the amount of time you are in class each day and week. In high school, you spent approximately six to eight hours per day in school, Monday through Friday. That totals between 30-40 hours per week. In college, you will spend approximately 15-18 hours per week in class, on average. This means you may have one or two courses per day. Depending on your schedule, you may not have any classes on certain days. This means you have a *lot* of time on your hands. How you spend this time will be a major factor in your academic success.

I'm always amazed how often students complain that they don't have enough time to accomplish things. When I ask them if they ever created a weekly schedule, they usually respond no. This is the first activity to help identify any issues with current time management skills.

There are two important things to understand in this section. First, if you are enrolled in 12 or more credit hours, school is your *full-time job*. A full-time job requires a minimum of 40 hours of work per week. This means at least 40 hours of your week should be dedicated to your studies. Let's assume that, on average, a full-time job requires about 45 hours per week (because most jobs require you to work a little overtime). Now, subtract the number of credit hours you are enrolled in this semester from 45. This will give you the minimum number of hours per week you should dedicate to studying. For example, if you are enrolled in 18 credit hours, then your minimum weekly study time should be 45-18=27 hours per week. While you may think this is a lot of time, think again. You will see below how it's not even skimming the surface.

Second, you must understand the difference between *priorities* and *non-priorities*. Priorities are activities that you *must* accomplish: eating, sleeping, bathing, exercising, studying, attending class, practice (if you received a scholarship that requires participation in an organization), or work (if you absolutely must have a job or work-study). Non-priorities are activities that you *want* to accomplish, but are not essential to your success at the university: extracurricular activities, parties, hanging out with friends, on or off-campus events, etc.

The following steps are outlined to help you develop or refine your time management skills. You may find that the steps below can initially be uncomfortable to complete. This is expected. You are now following a strict schedule that you are not accustomed to. However, the more you follow it, the easier it will become to accomplish each day.

1. *List all of your weekly priorities.* Again, these are activities that are essential to your success. Be sure that

you *only* include those activities that are necessities. Attending a football game, for example, only becomes a priority if you are a member of the team or other organization required to attend (e.g. cheerleader, pep band, etc.).

2. *Create a one-week calendar.* This calendar should include hourly slots for each day. For each activity identified above, enter the days and times for which they must be completed.

3. *Input non-priority activities, as permitted.* At this point, you should have a complete calendar for every priority you *must* accomplish in one week. Now, enter your non-priority activities, as your schedule permits. You won't be able to enter all of them, more than likely. That's ok. These aren't essential, so they will have to be done in moderation.

4. *Identify your less and more challenging courses.* You may excel in certain courses, while others require more effort. Categorizing your courses will help you prioritize your study time each week. This doesn't mean that courses in which you are currently excelling should be completely neglected for more challenging ones. Remember, your grade can change after any assignment or test. However, you may be able to dedicate more time more strategically each week.

5. *Utilize your weekends.* It's always great to have a break in your schedule. Make sure you utilize part of your weekend to review material. I used to give myself Saturdays off (unless there was a major project or exam the following week). Many times I had to, especially during basketball season, when we had Saturday games. Sunday evenings after dinner, I dedicated about 4-5 hours of study time to review material for the upcoming week, put finishing touches on any assignments, etc.

6. *Include some daily "me" time.* Your physical, mental, and emotional health is important to your academic success. To maintain it, find some daily "me" time. This may be 10-15 minutes or more per day. Do something that will help you decompress and regroup. Consider meditation, "quiet time" (no television, phone, or computer), exercise, or anything else you enjoy. You will find this short window of time helps you balance each day's activities.

After the same students who complained about not having enough time completed this activity, they were surprised to find that they had much more time in their schedules than they initially thought. Once you prioritize your activities, you still have time to accomplish some, if not all of your non-priority activities. Remember, everything can be done in moderation.

I was forced into developing good time management skills. In addition to practice once (and sometimes twice) a day, we had home and away games. Sometimes this meant I had to miss class. While professors will excuse absences due to university-related trips, you are still required to complete all assignments on time, and promptly make up any missed quizzes or tests. I had much less free time than most of my friends and classmates. I had to maximize my time to ensure that I not only stayed on top of my classes, but completed all of my other priorities as well.

Some of you may have additional priorities to consider, such as work, children, etc. It's even more important that you develop good time management skills. You also don't have the luxury of as much free time as some of your classmates. Balancing your schedule as early as possible ensures that you dedicate sufficient time to each priority in your life.

Once you have this calendar for one week, you can use it for each upcoming one, making slight modifications as necessary. After a few weeks of following this, it should become routine. I also found that creating daily tasks lists helped me identify anything that needed to be accomplished per day. It's important to note though, there are some things you may not fully complete. This is ok. If you have followed your proposed schedule, you will find a sense of gratification in accomplishing as many as you can.

Study Long and Prosper

Refining your study skills will help you maximize the 40+ hours of studying you accomplish each week. You may think that your current study skills are sufficient, especially if you excelled academically in high school. However, college is *very* different from high school. You have more free time and work. You are expected to learn and accomplish more in your courses, including reading, assignments, and projects.

No one is monitoring your studying in college. Your parents won't be there to make you study, nor are they controlling when and where you study. Just like time management, you should develop good study skills as early as possible to give yourself every advantage.

So how do you begin to develop better study skills? Like any other skill, you must continue to refine it. Learn from your mistakes and improve upon them each semester and year.

1. *Remove all distractions.* While many of us think we are excellent multi-taskers, the truth is that we are much less productive when there are numerous distractions. Think about it. How can you be sure that you fully understand integrals in Calculus when you are also trying to watch television? The first step in developing better study skills is to remove all unnecessary distractions. This includes phones, televisions, radio, MP3 players, computers (unless used to study), and friends. Also, if you must use your computer, then avoid non-class related websites. Sign off of instant messengers and social networks, to ensure you aren't distracted. If you find that you can't study in your room, then find distraction-free places around campus, such as quiet rooms in the library, computer labs, empty classrooms, etc.

2. *Determine your peak time.* This is the daily time period where you are the most productive. It's important to identify this time, and take advantage of it. Your weekly calendar should incorporate as much of your study time as possible into your peak time. Over my nine years in school, I learned that I am a night owl. During the day, my time is usually split balancing a number of things. It's often hard for me to sit down to study, work, write, or anything else. Emails, phone calls, errands, or even my favorite television show easily distracts me. I accomplish some work during the day, typically those things that don't require as much focus. Around 8pm though, I kick into overdrive. From about 8pm to 1am, I can accomplish a large amount of work. You should identify when you learn best. Once you do, make sure you maximize this time for studying.

3. *Participate in group study sessions wisely.* Study groups can sometimes be of great benefit. However, they can also be a major distraction. Think about the last time you met with a study group. All it takes is for one person to start a conversation about what happened last night, and the entire group is thrown off. In addition, everyone in the group may not be at the same level of comprehension in the course. For these reasons, study groups should be utilized cautiously. I always liked study groups for working on practice problems and material from class. However, prior to coming meetings, *everyone* in the group previously attempted to solve each problem. The group then became more productive, because everyone had input on each problem.

4. *Read and study prior to class.* This was discussed previously in chapter 3. It's important to reiterate that reading and studying your lecture notes before class is the best way to ensure that you stay on top of the material, are prepared to ask questions during class discussions, and do not have to cram before any exams. In high school, my mother would ask me nightly if I had

any homework. On the days when I didn't, I thought I would have an evening to myself. *WRONG*! Instead, she told me to review the material from class and the book, so that I was prepared for the next lesson. I continued this practice in college, and it made a world of difference in not only my performance in each class, but ultimately in the amount of free time I had throughout the semester. There was a reason that I could do all of the things I did and still maintain my GPA. I never had to worry about spending long hours in the library cramming for exams, because I was consistently studying each day throughout the semester.

Throughout this chapter, you've been provided with ways to develop and improve your organizational, time management, and study skills. These are critical to your academic success in college and beyond. In order to fully reap the benefits of these skills, you must practice them repeatedly. We've all heard the saying "practice makes perfect." Think about your favorite athletes. They must practice daily, and often for multiple hours per day, to excel. This is why they are the best. The same must apply to your academic pursuits. Your mind is a muscle. Just like any other muscle, it must be trained to improve. The more you train your mind, the better student you will become. I tell my students each semester, excelling academically is not about what you know, but how hard you are willing to work to learn what you don't know. How hard are you working?

Step Six

Search for Financial Aid Until You Have a Zero Balance

I was recently interviewed about the rise in student loan debt and its cause. While there are a number of obvious factors to attribute it to, such as rising tuition rates, the truth is that part of this is due to the choices of students and parents. You may think this is a little harsh, but consider this. I recently advertised a scholarship opportunity for freshman in five departments across the School of Engineering. The scholarship ranged from $4000-8000 per year for two years. The only requirement was a simple application, essay, and proof of unmet financial need. We advertised to approximately 100 students. We received a total of six applications. During this same time, I advertised a scholarship opportunity to rising juniors. For two years, they would receive a $10,000 scholarship and $400/month stipend per year. There were three scholarships available. One student applied. Do you see where I'm going with this?

Every semester, I encounter students who are in desperate need of financial aid. These students often don't search for and apply to scholarships throughout the academic year until it's too late and they've acquired student loan debt. As a high-school senior, students (and parents) are often so overwhelmed and frustrated with the college application process that they neglect searching diligently for financial aid. When asked why they don't apply to more scholarships, most students respond that they don't want to complete the essay or personal statement. As a result, they forfeit thousands of dollars in scholarships, because they don't want to write a 500-word essay.

I recently read an article about a young man who was entering his freshman year of college. He'd received over $300,000 in scholarships as a high-school senior. He didn't have some special circumstances. As a high-school freshman, his mother told him the only way he could attend college was by winning scholarships or joining the military. He knew that he didn't want to join the military, so he began to research scholarships for the next four years. There was no magic formula to his success. He started early and was diligent.

Think about your senior year of high school. How committed were you to finding financial aid? Did you apply to any and every scholarship possible, or did you find a few and stop once you received your student award letter from the university? Do you have a student loan? Have you been as diligent as you should be as an undergraduate? If you're honest, many of you will admit that you didn't exhaust your financial aid search. There is one problem with this: like any other loan, student loans *must* be repaid! This means you and your parents will be responsible for this expense once you graduate, if not sooner.

If you did not receive a full scholarship, this is an important chapter for you to read. Your search for financial aid should *not* stop until the amount you owe for your college education is $0. This means that you must find non-repayment forms of financial aid.

Non-Repayment Forms of Financial Aid

There are three main forms of financial aid that require no repayment.

Scholarships

Scholarships are categorized as need or merit-based. Need-based scholarships are awarded to students demonstrating a financial need for assistance in paying for college expenses, as determined by the Free Application for Federal Student Aid (FAFSA). Merit-based scholarships are awarded based on the student's achievement in academics, athletics, or any other area identified by the granting organization.

Grants

Grants are awarded from a number of sources and are based on varying circumstances, including need, age, race, intended major or university, disability, etc. Some of the most common grants include the Pell Grant, Academic Competitiveness Grant, and Teacher Education Assistance for College and Higher Education (TEACH) Grant.

Work Study
These programs provide financial compensation to students who complete university-based work assignments for a maximum of 20 hours per week. Work assignments can vary across the campus. If you qualify for federal work study, this will be noted on your Student Aid Report.

Complete the FAFSA Every Year
The first mistake many students make is assuming that the FAFSA is only important when applying to colleges and universities. This is a *MAJOR* misconception. The FAFSA is only valid for *one* academic year. You must complete it every year that you are enrolled. The FAFSA is used to determine your Expected Family Contribution (EFC), which determines your financial need for the upcoming academic year. Your EFC determines what federal or state-based aid, including need-based scholarships, grants, and work-study that you qualify for. In case you don't remember, your EFC is the amount that you and your family can contribute to your college education. Your need is determined as

Need=Cost of Attendance-EFC

The university uses your need to create your financial aid package. This includes scholarships, grants, work-study, and student loans. Each year that you are enrolled, you (and your parents) must complete the FAFSA between January 1 and June 30. It's important that you submit the FAFSA as early as possible. The priority deadline for your university and state will vary. Be sure your parents also complete their income tax returns as early as possible. Your FAFSA application is not processed until these have been accepted.

Apply to Every Scholarship You Find

You will inevitably have to balance your academic studies with other activities and requirements. Hopefully, you developed better time management and organizational skills after reading chapter 4. This means that, while attending classes, studying, and more, you should find and apply to every scholarship opportunity possible. Maintain your profile on scholarship databases such as FastWeb, CollegeNet, and ScholarMatch. You can also find scholarship opportunities through your department, school/college, and university.

Many students don't know this, but there are a number of unsolicited scholarships that are often available. Each year, our department receives emails and calls from organizations requesting that we nominate a student to receive a scholarship. The nominated student has no application to complete or transcript to submit. It's as simple as answering "yes" or "no." This is why it's important to have a good relationship with your professors, attend class regularly (and on time), submit assignments, ask for help if needed, and be known for the right reasons. We discussed this in chapter 3. Finally, if a scholarship requires a letter of recommendation, be sure to request it at least two weeks prior to the deadline. You should also provide the individual providing the recommendation with a copy of your resume.

Maintain a Competitive GPA

In addition to scholarship opportunities, a competitive GPA is important when pursuing internships, job opportunities, and graduate school. Your goal should be to maintain a 3.0 or better each year. It's pretty hard to justify recommending a student for a scholarship when his/her GPA is below a 3.0. Most academic scholarships have a minimum GPA requirement to receive and maintain the award.

Find University-Based Financial Aid

Once you are enrolled at the university, you will find a number of additional funding opportunities that you qualify for as a current student.

Teaching Assistantships (TA)

These students assist professors with a specific course. TAs may hold office hours, study sessions, help with labs, or grade assignments.

Research Assistantships (RA)

These students work with professors on research projects. Many professors have grants to perform research. There is often funding for student support included. Your responsibilities can vary in this type of position. One of the benefits of this position is that you will gain not only financial support, but invaluable experience as an undergraduate researcher. This looks great on your resume, especially if you plan to attend graduate school.

Lab Assistantships and Tutors

Lab assistants are responsible for setting up and maintaining any labs, and assisting with any issues that arise. Tutors are responsible for helping other students better understand material in one or more courses. You can find these opportunities throughout most campuses. If you excel in a specific subject, this is an excellent opportunity to consider.

These opportunities will not be automatically awarded in your financial aid package. To be considered for any of these, you must not only actively seek them out, but also perform well academically. To learn about the opportunities available at your university, speak to your professors, department chair, and office of student services.

Defer Student Loan Payments

IF you have to accept a student loan, then choose to defer your payments until you graduate. This means that you don't have to begin repaying the loan until after you graduate (or stop attending college). Once you defer your student loan payments, use any financial aid you receive throughout the academic year (e.g. scholarships, grants, TA/RA positions, etc.) to minimize the loan amount. This will help you get closer to your $0 balance and minimize the amount you owe upon graduation.

If you receive any support in the form of direct payment to you (e.g. student loan refund check, stipend, work-study, etc.), then use this to pay down your student loans. I remember classmates who received student loan refund checks and spent it on clothes and shoes. Unfortunately, they didn't realize that they were going to have to pay *that* money back as well.

Seek Assistance

I recently received an email from a student who informed me (the week before the first day of classes) that she would be withdrawing from the university for the semester, due to financial issues. She'd been living with a relative, who would no longer be able to house her. Since her family couldn't afford tuition *and* on-campus housing, she felt her best option was to withdraw and hopefully return in the spring semester.

Had she contacted me one week earlier, she would've been able to circumvent this issue. There were numerous financial aid opportunities available for students with unmet need in the department (including the one I previously mentioned that very few students applied to). Unfortunately, we did not know of her situation because she didn't inform us until she'd already made the decision. This was a good student, who was entering her sophomore year with a 3.4 GPA. By the time she notified me, she'd already withdrawn for the semester, and could not enroll again. Fortunately, she remained in contact with us, returned to the university, and is thriving. Everyone's story doesn't have a happy ending like this one.

Before you make any decisions to withdraw or transfer from the university, be sure to speak to your department chair, advisor, and office of student services. There may be financial aid opportunities that you are not aware of. The key is that you must inform someone. If you feel like this is an embarrassing situation for you to discuss, then here is some comforting news: *YOU ARE NOT ALONE.* As the cost of tuition continues to rise across the country, many students and families are finding it difficult to afford the cost of attendance. Never let this deter you from asking for help. It is our job as faculty and staff to help you succeed.

In addition to applying for financial aid, be sure that you also monitor your financial aid status each year. This will help you track the amount of aid received and your remaining unmet need. Remember, until you have a $0 balance, you should exhaust all options. Maximize your "down-time" in your weekly schedule (including weekends and summers) and apply, apply, *APPLY*! Remember, receiving financial aid is similar to winning the lottery: you have to be in it to win it!

Step Seven

Learn and Practice Money-Management Skills

The truth is that most of us want to make money. The more education you have, the more money you will make over your lifetime. A report by the U.S. Census Bureau determined that, over the course of a working adult's lifetime, high-school graduates will earn approximately $1.2 million, compared to college graduates earning $2.1 million. For those with graduate and professional degrees, the earnings increase. This illustrates that the more education you have, the more money you can expect to make. Now get to studying!

Whether your goal is to be rich, comfortable, or you really don't care about money, the truth is you will *need* it to live in this world. Just as you are learning about your discipline, you should begin learning how to manage and spend your money now, so you won't have any problems once you *really* start making it.

Disclaimer: I'm not a financial advisor. However, I graduated from college and graduate school with no debt (other than a mortgage) and investments. Hopefully, you can accomplish the same by following these steps.

Set Financial Goals

Have you thought about your 5, 10, and 15-year financial goals? Probably not. The truth is that most college students don't give serious thought to this. If you are reading this, then you have the opportunity to be more financially aware and prepared than those of us who came before you. You've probably envisioned your future to include a number of great things, but how are you going to get there? What will it take to achieve your goals?

The first step to achieving any goal is to establish it. You must begin planning your path to success now because, as surprisingly ridiculous as it seems, the choices you make now will impact the rest of your life. Did you catch the sarcasm in there? If so, great! If not, time to wake up. In order to reach a destination, you must have a roadmap to follow. To help you identify and set your financial goals, answer the following questions:

1. *Where do you see yourself in 5, 10, and 15 years?*
2. *What type of lifestyle do you want to have?*
3. *What city do you plan to live in?*
4. *Will you have student loan or other debt when you graduate?*

In 5 years, you will be a recent grad, either working in your career (hopefully) or in graduate school. In 10 or 15 years, your lifestyle will probably change. Will you start a family, own a home, or start your own business? The lifestyle you desire will cost money. Do you want a dream home or car? Do you want to travel multiple times per year? What city will you live in? The cost of living can differ drastically depending on what part of the country or world you reside in. In addition, your income may vary depending on location. Finally, if you incur any debt upon graduation, part of your income will be dedicated to repaying this.

One of the biggest mistakes recent college graduates make is living above their means once they land that great career. Having a nice car, home, and being able to spend money on whatever they chose trumps making wise financial decisions that will help them maintain a comfortable lifestyle for life. Begin setting financial goals now and planning your path to achieving them before graduation.

Understand and Value Good Credit

When I was in college, there were so many credit card companies with tables in the student union during the first week of class that it resembled a career fair. Students were enticed to apply for credit cards with a number of "free" gifts. Some students took the bait without fully understanding credit, the responsibility that comes with using it, and the consequences of any irresponsibility. Some students ended up thousands of dollars in debt with a bad credit history before they graduated. They opened credit cards, began spending money on everything and nothing, and eventually found out that the money they borrowed had to be repaid. Unfortunately, they didn't think about that beforehand.

Do you have a classmate who is already in credit card debt? Do you own a credit card? Were you taught about credit and how to properly use it? It is important that you read and re-read this chapter yearly, monthly, weekly, and daily, if necessary. Discuss your thoughts and questions with classmates, instructors, parents, mentors, credit counseling agencies, and others who can help you become informed and responsible before you establish and use credit.

Another disclaimer: this chapter is not designed to be a comprehensive guide to credit. It is designed to provide you with information on how to make wise decisions regarding money and credit, so that you can avoid making the same mistakes that others have made. Remember, the choices you make now can positively or negatively impact your future. Give yourself every opportunity to win.

The simplest definition of credit is *the level of confidence that a borrower will repay a loan*. Remember that you will need money to live in this world. There is a strong likelihood that you won't be able to pay cash for everything you will need or want. For example, that new car you want when you graduate may cost $25,000. That 3-bedroom condo with a view in the city may cost $300,000.

Where will you get the money to make such expensive purchases? This is where credit comes into the picture. Let's consider a small example. You want to purchase an airline ticket home for the holidays and found an inexpensive flight online.

You may use your credit card to book the flight. These are all examples of purchases on credit. You, the borrower, are lent money to make the purchase from a lender, on the condition that you promise to pay the money back plus interest. This interest is considered your fee for borrowing the money. You will be responsible for paying the money back, plus interest, in a monthly fee until your debt has been paid in full.

Think about when a friend asks you if he can borrow a shirt. In this case, you (the lender) are providing your shirt with the understanding that he (the borrower) will pay you $5 per month, until the shirt is returned to you. The shirt was what your friend (the borrower) needed. However, you (the lender) charge your friend for the opportunity to use your shirt, until it is returned to you. Borrowers are lent money for various purchases, on the condition that they promise to repay it later. In addition to repaying the loan, they must also pay a fee for the opportunity to use the money, known as the interest or finance charge.

A lender is usually a person, financial institution, or business that provides money to borrowers. How much they charge you to borrow the money is based on a number of factors, including the purpose of the loan and your credit score. Did you or your parents obtain any student loans for your college expenses? If so, your student loans are another example of purchasing on credit. You borrowed money from the government (federal student loans) or a financial institution in order to pay for the cost of attendance at your university. You are expected to repay this money and also the interest, which is your fee for borrowing the money.

Know Your Credit Score

Let's assume that the first month after your friend borrowed your shirt, he forgot to pay you the monthly $5 charge. The next month, the payment was late, and it was only $3. In the third month, you didn't receive any payment. You are going to be very upset with your friend, probably decide that this was a bad decision to lend him the shirt, and vow never to do that again!

A credit score is used to determine your creditworthiness, how much confidence a lender can have that you will repay your loan as promised. Credit scores are based on your credit report, which is a detailed list of all loans you have received and your corresponding payment history. Your friend, for example, would have negative information on his credit report from you. Depending on what other information is on his credit report, his credit score would be negatively affected.

There are three major credit bureaus that each calculate a credit score for you: Equifax, TransUnion, and Experian. Credit scores range from 300-850. The higher your credit score, the better.

If you want to rent an apartment and, in some cases, qualify for certain jobs, your credit history will be checked. Your credit history is a financial label that informs lenders and other institutions how much confidence they should have in your ability to repay any loan. You want anyone to have as much confidence as possible in your abilities don't you? You should also want to be viewed as very trustworthy or creditworthy. Any information on your credit report will impact your credit score either positively or negatively. If most of the items on your report are positive, then you will typically have a higher credit score. The more negative items that are present, the lower your credit score will be. Borrowers with higher credit scores are viewed as more creditworthy and usually receive larger loan amounts with lower interest rates. Those with lower credit scores are viewed as less creditworthy and will have more trouble finding lenders who will lend them money. Any loans they do receive will usually have much higher interest rates. This is because these borrowers are viewed as much larger risks (remember your friend and the shirt).

There are a number of important things you should know and practice, especially as a college student:

1. *Do not establish any credit unless you have thoroughly discussed it with your parents.* One of the first things my parents told me when I entered college was *DO NOT*

OPEN ANY CREDIT CARDS!! They did not want me to make poor financial decisions and end up in debt that I could not afford to repay. I understand that sometimes a credit card may be necessary, such as for emergencies. However, you should first discuss having an emergency credit card with your parents. If you feel like you need to speak to a credit-counseling agency, then there are plenty that will provide free counseling. Many credit card companies have options for parents to add you as an additional cardholder. This will allow you to have access to an emergency card, with your parents able to monitor and track any spending.

2. *Make payments monthly and on time.* If you are only using your card for emergencies (e.g. travel home, car repairs, etc.) then pay the balance off at the end of the month, if possible. If not, pay the balance off as quickly as possible. The longer it takes you to repay the loan, the more interest you will be charged. If you do not pay at least the monthly minimum or on time, then your credit score can be negatively impacted.

3. *Maintain low balance-to-limit ratios.* Let's assume you have a new credit card with a limit of $10,000. You paid for unexpected car repairs that totaled $500. Your balance-to-limit ratio is $500/$10,000, or 5% [(500/10000)*100]. The lower this ratio is, the better your credit score will be. Try to keep your balance on any credit card lower than 25% of the limit. A larger balance-to-limit ratio means that you are borrowing too much money on credit, which is a red flag to lenders.

4. *Obtain a copy of your credit report yearly.* You can order a free copy of your credit reports from each of the three agencies once per year. If there are any mistakes on your credit report, contact the credit bureau and lender to correct them. Be aware that this may take time.

During my senior year of college, I discussed with my parents that I opened an Express store credit card, with a very small limit. I used it to make a few small purchases throughout the year, and always paid the balance in full at the end of the month I made the purchase. This helped me to build my credit. However, I made responsible decisions to only use the card infrequently, as a means to help build my credit. If you are interested in establishing credit, then you should first discuss it with your parents and anyone else that can help you an informed decision. Establishing credit does not mean you must make purchases every month using your credit card, nor does it mean you should make large purchases. It means you must show that you are creditworthy.

Open a Bank Account

As a child, I would often accompany my mother while she shopped. There was one time that I wanted her to buy something and she said no. In a confused state, I asked, "why can't you just write a check?" I should acknowledge that this was the 1980's. There were no debit cards, so people used to checks to pay from their checking accounts. From my observation (and child-like ignorance), checks replaced money. As long as you had a check to write, you could purchase whatever you wanted!

When I was 12, my parents opened a personal savings account for me. I used this to deposit any Christmas, birthday, or random money I received. I remember being so excited about my new responsibility. I even had my own ATM card, and learned how to track my expenses, monitor my savings, and calculate any interest earned on my account.

When I entered college, I kept this same account, and used it for my personal spending money. I was surprised that many students didn't have bank accounts. If they needed money, someone wired it to them via Western Union. This meant that there was a $10-$20 fee every time they were sent money. While it may not seem like a lot of money, these fees add up. As a college student, think about what you could use $20 to pay for!

Regardless of what university you attend, there should be a local bank or credit union near campus. You can usually open a savings or checking account with as little as $5. If you've never had a bank account before, start with a simple savings account. Some banks and credit unions have special accounts and rates for college students. Monitor and track your money, including low balances. Later, open a checking account if you feel comfortable using a debit card or checks. If anyone needs to send you money, have it deposited into your account. This will save you hundreds of dollars per year in wire fees.

Set and Follow a Budget

If you haven't already done so, you *must* create a budget immediately. Why would you need a budget in college? Most students have a minimal amount of money to spend. If you live on campus, most, if not all of your living expenses are pre-paid through room and board. However, you still need money for books, supplies, and miscellaneous expenses (e.g. food, entertainment, etc.). If you live off campus, then you are aware of the numerous monthly expenses you incur. In either case, a budget is important for a few reasons. First, it will help you develop fiscal discipline and responsibility. Second, it will help you learn to live within (and preferably below) your means.

There are a few simple steps to help you create and follow your budget. You can modify or add steps as you see fit. However, the key is to begin to practice financial discipline that will help you reach the goals that you set.

1. *List all monthly expenses.* Beside each expense, list how frequently you make this purchase (daily, weekly, monthly, rarely). This will help you identify your spending habits. Add all amounts. These are your total monthly expenses.

2. *List all sources of income.* Income is considered any money that you receive (e.g. work-study, stipends, money from home, student loan refund, etc.). List all income in a second column, including how frequently you receive it (e.g. per week, month, quarter, semester, etc.) Do not include any money that you do not receive on a consistent basis (e.g. a one-time payment for selling a pair of shoes). Add all amounts. This is the total

amount of expected income. Your total expenses should be significantly lower than your total income. If it isn't, then you have a lot of budgeting to do!

3. *Identify each necessity.* Remember there is a difference between necessities and wants. *Necessities* are things that you require to live and function. Depending on whether you live on or off campus, your necessities may vary. For example, if you live on campus, your necessities may include books, toiletries, money for washing clothes, etc. If you live off campus, your necessities may include rent or mortgage, utilities, transportation fees to/from campus, and food. *Wants* are things such as entertainment (e.g. money for parties, events, etc.), clothes, and eating out. List your necessities and wants in separate columns on the same sheet. Total the amount in each column. If your total expenses are higher than your total necessities, this means you are spending money on things you don't need!!

4. *Pay yourself first.* Whatever income you receive, put 10% aside for yourself in some form of savings. There are a number of options that you can use in addition to a savings account. You can speak to a representative at any bank or a financial advisor on these options.

5. *Keep a "funny money" limit.* This is a small amount of money that you allow yourself to spend however you choose. Once this amount is spent each week or month, you are no longer able to spend any money on wants. This will help you moderate your excess spending and identify how to spread the fun out as well.

Spend Your Money Wisely

When I was a kid, my parents would tell me that money would burn a hole through my pockets. I absolutely *had* to spend it. Usually, it was on something that was a want (and a waste). Does money burn a hole in your pockets? Are you spending money wisely? Have you set and followed a budget that allows you to not only pay your monthly expenses, but also pay yourself?

When I was in college, I interned every summer at IBM. This was considered an extremely great position, especially since IBM paid computer science interns *VERY* well! Each week, I deposited this money into my bank account, allowing myself a little money to spend during the summer. When I returned to school, I had a nice amount of savings that allowed me to handle all of my necessities and wants during the school year. Since I had no student loans, this money was available to use at my discretion.

Thankfully I developed fiscal discipline and had no student loan or credit card debt. I also had minimal expenses, since I lived on campus. My only regret is that I did not learn more about investments (including paying myself first) at that time, to begin building my personal portfolio. I did not know anything about the types of investment opportunities and how this money could help me later on in life. Learn about and take advantage of any opportunities to invest your money wisely, starting now. You will thank yourself later!

Step Eight

Participate in Internships, Co-ops or Other Experiences

Again, I ask the question, what is the real reason you are in college? Your answer (at least after reading the first seven chapters, at this point) should be to obtain a successful career in your field. So what does it take to land your "dream job?" Passing your classes? Yes. Great GPA? Probably. But it takes a little bit more than that. Of course, grades are important, but there are other factors that also play a part in making you "marketable." Depending on your major, the criteria can vary. For many careers, experience is important.

Regardless of your major or post-graduation goals, there are a few things you should consider.

Grades Aren't Everything

In class, you will learn theoretical concepts. These are fundamentals that you will need throughout your academic and professional career. They will serve as the foundation for everything you do in your field. However, employers and even graduate schools look for individuals who also have experience applying these fundamentals outside of the classroom. These opportunities allow you to not only apply your classroom knowledge, but also gain practical experience dealing with the real-world context of all of that "book stuff" that many students think is never used.

You Must Set Yourself Apart

Remember when you were applying to colleges and universities? There were millions of high-school graduates doing the same thing. What set you apart from the rest of the competition? Fast-forward to your current undergraduate studies.

There are plenty of other undergraduates applying to jobs and graduate school. Just like with college admissions, you aren't competing with just your peers around the world. You are also competing with individuals who are currently working and looking for a career change or to pursue graduate studies. What sets you apart from everyone else applying? You may be the top student at your current institution. However, you are competing with a pool of applicants who are as equally talented, if not more. Remembering this will help you stay as competitive as possible.

Identify Careers You Like...or Don't Like

I majored in computer science because I loved to program. However, it was only after completing a few summer internships that I realized, while I love to program, sitting in front of a computer all day and not interacting with people wasn't the best career move for me. Gaining this real-world experience will allow you to not only identify your strengths and weaknesses, but also what you like to do, love to do, and would prefer to never do again in life. This can help you avoid entering a career that you would never be happy in, versus one that is the perfect fit for you.

You obtain this experience through opportunities such as internships, co-ops, and research opportunities. Speak to your advisor and department chair to learn which of these is the most appropriate and advantageous for you.

Internships

Internships allow students to participate in on-the-job training at an organization for a specific time period. Most internships are full or part-time positions that occur during the summer break. The positions may be paid or unpaid. During this period, you are considered an employee of the company. You will work on one or more assignments that allow you to apply your theoretical classroom knowledge. In addition to work assignments, many employers provide activities for interns, including outings and events, professional development workshops, and more.

The goal of any internship is to obtain exposure to a specific career, employer, company culture, and more. One of the benefits of an internship is that they typically occur during the summer break. Unless you plan to attend summer school, they do not interrupt your studies. Many companies will invite students to return in the subsequent summer, pending a successful experience. However, there is no requirement that you work for the company in subsequent summers or upon graduation. You have the option to choose where you intern.

There are a few important things to note about internships. As mentioned before, positions may be paid or unpaid. While every student would love to be paid, the truth is that not everyone will. This is usually based on your major and intended career. For example, internships in disciplines such as communications and public relations may be unpaid. This is due to the fact that there are many more students (and potential graduates) in these fields than there are post-graduation opportunities. Employers will offer unpaid internships, assuming that the experience is valuable enough to help build your professional portfolio. *Do not* turn down an opportunity because it is unpaid, especially if this is common in your discipline. Remember, employers look for what sets candidates apart from the competition when evaluating for post-graduation opportunities.

Second, depending on the field, location, and required experience, certain employers will pay more competitively than others. For these positions, employers often consider the most competitive students who demonstrate the ability to excel both inside and outside of the classroom. Make sure you understand this while searching for and applying to opportunities.

Finally, depending on the size of the company, there may be other interns working with you. This is a great time to network and meet students from other schools across the world. Remember, you all will be entering the workforce or graduate school around the same time. It's great to have a network of colleagues to share your experiences with. I'm forever grateful to the friends I met during my summer internships, many of whom I'm friends with to this day.

Co-ops

Cooperative education experiences (co-ops) are partnerships between the student, university, and employer. Like internships, students participate in on-the-job training. This experience is designed to gain real-world experience in a specific area, with a specific employer, or both. However, there are a few differences between internships and co-ops.

First, co-op experiences may be completed for academic credit, pay, or both. Second, students typically complete a co-op over the course of one or more semesters. If participating in a co-op, you are considered a full-time employee at the company. You will not be enrolled in classes during the semester(s) that you are employed. Since you aren't enrolled in consecutive semesters, it's important to note that you may not graduate on the same schedule as your classmates. However, there is a significant trade-off in participating in a co-op.

The goal of a co-op is not only to gain real-world experience, but also to obtain a full-time position with a company upon graduation. While you may take longer to graduate, the sponsoring company usually hires you upon graduation. This can be a great incentive, especially considering the job market in your field.

Research Opportunities and Summer Programs

If you are considering attending graduate school, you should definitely identify opportunities to participate in undergraduate research, either during the school year or the summer. During a research opportunity, students work with a university faculty member on a research project. These opportunities can be paid or unpaid. Students can participate in a research experience during the academic year at their home institution or during the summer at their home or another institution.

You may have the opportunity to publish a research paper and/or present your work at a conference in your discipline. The goal of a research experience is to gain hands-on experience in your field, understand and implement the research process, and prepare for graduate studies.

The first place to look for research opportunities is within your department. Ask your department chair and professors about their research interests and any opportunities to work with them. Again, it is important to note that while you may not receive a stipend, you *will* gain invaluable experience. Remember, the end justifies the means. In order to reach your ultimate goal, you will have to do certain things along the way that are different than what you originally expected or desired.

Advice for Successful Experiences

Now that you understand the types of experience available as an undergraduate, it's important that you participate in at least one per academic year in order to be as competitive as possible upon graduation. Whatever opportunity you select, make sure you remember the following points to ensure a successful experience (and hopefully a job offer or acceptance letter):

1. *Do your job well.* Whatever you're assigned, complete it above expectation. Leave your supervisors with a positive image of you.

2. *Become a sponge.* Ask questions, especially if you don't know something. It's ok to ask for help. In addition, learn as much as you can and soak it all up.

3. *Talk to colleagues.* You will have co-workers, supervisors, and probably a mentor. Develop a relationship with them. They each have valuable information to share on their experience and what you can do to best prepare yourself for a career.

4. *Complete weekly progress reports.* This will serve multiple purposes. First, you will be able to update your supervisors on your weekly activities. Second, you will be able to add this information to your professional portfolio of accomplishments.

5. *Ask for more work.* If you complete an assignment, ask for another. Supervisors love to see this...trust me.

6. *Be professional.* You are at work. Dress the part (whatever that is in your field). If you are provided equipment (e.g. computers, phone, etc.), refrain from using them for personal reasons, such as social media or personal conversations.

7. *Work on your presentation and writing skills.* This is something that all students need but few properly develop. Take advantage of opportunities to speak in front of a group and write. These are valued skills in the workplace.

8. *Accept feedback.* Develop a thick skin, and learn to accept constructive criticism as a means for professional development.

9. *Find a mentor.* If you weren't assigned one, ask someone you are comfortable with to serve as one for you. If you have one but aren't comfortable with him/her, identify another individual to serve as a second mentor.

10. *Maximize the opportunity.* Remember you are there to learn, work, and have fun! Do all of these!

11. *Step outside of your comfort zone.* These opportunities may not be in your hometown or near your university. Don't be afraid to travel to new places and create new experiences.

12. *Don't waste a summer.* You should be participating in one of these opportunities each summer. You should *NOT* go home and find a job in the mall, for example. Each summer should be spent applying the foundation you learned in the classroom to real-world problems. Remember, you need to set yourself apart from the competition.

Step Nine

Understand the Road Ahead As a First-Generation College Student

When I originally began this book, I foolishly neglected to consider a chapter dedicated to first-generation college students. I wanted every chapter to be of benefit to any student. However, as time progressed (and it took me longer than anticipated to complete it), I quickly realized that it would be remiss of me to not dedicate a chapter to students who are the first in their family to attend college. Their journey can include a number of unique challenges and it's important that students understand these beforehand to hopefully avoid some of them.

I recently read an article about three young ladies from Texas who were first-generation college students. The trio grew up in a community where few attended college. They were always the top three students in their class, and continuously pushed each other throughout elementary, middle, and high school. All three students were supported by teachers and guidance counselors who recognized and nurtured their academic potential.

It was no surprise when these young ladies graduated at the top of their class. However, from that point, the story didn't read as I expected. All three students pursued a post-secondary education. College, however, proved to be a completely different world for each of them: a world that, no matter how talented they were academically, they were drastically unprepared to enter. One young lady was late to register for the academic year at her university, including housing, classes, and completing the FAFSA. Because she didn't know what to do or where to begin during the preceding summer, she spent her freshman year playing catch-up and accepting student loans to cover the expensive cost of attendance at the university. As she progressed through her freshman year, she struggled in courses in her intended major. In her second year, the university erroneously miscalculated her EFC as higher than it was, making her ineligible for much-needed financial aid. She was forced to accept more student loans to cover the expenses of her sophomore year. The young lady eventually dropped out of college and is working in her hometown.

The second young lady struggled to balance her new life as a college student with her old friends from home, including a boyfriend who was not in college, frequently unemployed, and developing a costly drug habit. In an effort to maintain her relationship, she moved off campus into an apartment with her boyfriend, and ran up her credit cards to support her living expenses. After nearly losing her financial aid due to poor academic performance, this young lady eventually left her boyfriend and managed to improve academically. She is now a fifth-year senior, expected to graduate soon, albeit with a large amount of student loan and credit card debt.

The third young lady decided to attend a community college in her hometown. Fearing she was betraying her family by leaving, she convinced herself that this was her best and only option. Even when family members encouraged her to attend a four-year institution away from home, she convinced herself that it wasn't the best time to leave, given certain family situations. She successfully completed her associate's degree. However, she is working at a bar in her hometown.

The story of these three young ladies is all too common for too many students. There are a number of pressures and uncertainties that first-generation college students face. Knowing what is ahead of you will not only help you properly prepare for any hiccups along the way, but also eliminate the element of surprise, which is often followed by frustration and, in some unfortunate cases, leaving the university without a degree.

First, it is important to note that college is a major adjustment for *every* student. Regardless of your ethnicity, gender, socio-economic level, or first-generation status, this is probably your first time away from home. You are expected to undertake a large amount of responsibility for your academic and professional success, all at the age of 17 or 18 for most of you. Students whose parents are college graduates can refer to them for assistance or directions on how to best navigate through this maze. For first-generation college students, this experience is new for both you and your family. This uncertainty and expectation can be frustrating and overwhelming. However, it should not be a deterrent.

Find an On-Campus Advocate

In *Prepped for Success*, you learned how to create a team of individuals that is genuinely vested in your college admissions success. You must find at least one person on campus that serves a similar purpose. This person can be a professor, administrator, or staff member. The important thing is that this person is not only knowledgeable of the university and what it takes to be successful, but also willing to take you under his/her wing to ensure that you have what you need and are also performing to the highest expectations. I call this person an accountability partner.

Your accountability partner ensures that you uphold your end of the bargain, which is successfully completing college. He/she will assist you as needed. However, you must do your part. Find this person early, and maintain a relationship. I've found myself inadvertently becoming this advocate for students since I began teaching. It's usually not because they approached me, but because I recognized their potential and realized their need for someone to serve this purpose. If you make yourself known within your department, you will soon find that people will take a genuine interest in you, regardless of your academic performance, classification, or request.

Get to Know the Right People

It was discussed in chapter 3 why your department chair, advisor, and professors are critical to your academic future. They can also help you personally and professionally. You would be surprised how many professors have stories similar to yours. Be sure that they know you, for the right reasons. They may be able to offer advice, funding or professional opportunities, and more. In addition, identify the university or school's Office of Student Services. This office is designed to help students with a range of areas, including financial aid, career counseling, and academic support.

Know and Monitor Your Financial Aid Status

There should be *NO* surprises when it comes to your financial aid. Most universities allow you to access your financial account via an online student web portal. If you have questions or concerns, contact your financial aid office. Here is my personal advice regarding financial aid offices: *SPEAK TO SOMEONE, NOT THEIR VOICEMAIL*! This office is responsible for all students at the university. Voicemails don't always get checked. If no one answers, leave a message, email, and *CALL BACK*. Then call back again, and again, and again, and make a personal visit to the office if you have to. Remember, the squeaky wheel gets the oil. Once you have spoken to someone, follow this with an email to confirm and document the conversation.

Become a Pest

This may not sound like the best advice but the truth is exactly what I said above: the squeaky wheel gets the oil. It is in your best interest to be known, for the right reasons. I can't say this enough. People remember the students they always see. Whether it's coming to office hours, asking or answering questions in class, checking on your financial aid status, or inquiring about upcoming recruiting events and opportunities, students who do these things are more likely to receive unsolicited assistance during their college years. So stay in the forefront of everyone's mind. Remember, you are the customer. We are all here to ensure your academic success.

Ask for Help

It's ok to *not* know something. However, you will never receive the correct answer or assistance if you don't let people know that you *need* help. Now is not the time to be proud. In fact, you are expected to not know certain things when you begin your college experience. For example, how would you know the registration process for classes as an incoming freshman without your advisor's assistance? The same applies for things such as financial aid, meal plans, etc. To help, start by asking the following questions:

1. *Where do I find information on my major and course requirements?*
2. *How do I add/drop courses? When are the time periods for this each semester?*
3. *How do I view/track my financial aid? How do I find additional funding?*
4. *What are the requirements to maintain my financial aid?*
5. *Where do I view and update my meal plan?*
6. *Who are my advisor and department chair? What do they need from me?*
7. *Is there any additional information I need to know as a student?*

If you don't know the correct answer to each of these questions, then you ask where you can find it. Remember, it's ok to ask for help. However, you also have to help yourself. This is another step in your academic accountability.

Keep Positive People Around

There was a cell phone commercial a few years ago that asked, "Who's in your five?" The ad offered unlimited calls to customers' five most-frequently called numbers. I use this phrase and commercial frequently when I speak to students, because it has a much greater meaning than originally implied. The people closest to you are often the biggest influences in your life. Who are the five closest people to you? Do they provide positive influences, reinforcement, encouragement, and peer pressure? If not, then you need to identify a way to move them from your "five" to another, less intimate circle or network in your life.

This includes family, friends, and significant others. College is a major accomplishment! Remember, it is something to be proud of. There are times when those around you may not understand or appreciate this. They may not understand that you can't come home every weekend to visit, or that when you are home, you have to study and do school work. Do not let these things and people deter you.

You an Extraordinary Thing

This is something to celebrate, not belittle or downplay. You have earned the opportunity to further pursue your education. Always view this as an extraordinary opportunity that you have been fortunate enough to take advantage of. *NEVER* take this for granted.

Stay Informed

You may be a first-generation college student. However, you are *still* a college student. You are expected to be responsible for your academic success. Make sure that you are always on top of everything academically and financially.

Keep Your Family Informed

The FAFSA and other forms, such as housing, may require family-related information. You must remember to stay on your family to complete them. Students have lost housing because their parents didn't submit their room deposit before the deadline. Make sure you *and* your family all aware of all required documents and deadlines.

College is Not High School.

This should be self-explanatory at this point. You are responsible for doing your assignments on time, attending class (on time), and anything else. There is no hand holding. Remember this and act accordingly.

Homesickness is Normal

My first few months of college were an adjustment. Yours will probably be too. However, it's important to remember that succeeding in college requires properly adjusting to college life. With modern technology, you can keep in touch with your family and friends via phone, email, video chat, and social networks. Use these as much as possible to help you adjust to your new home. You may find that, after one semester, your homesickness significantly declines. Mine completely disappeared!

Avoid Majoring in the Minors

One of the biggest downfalls for college students is spreading themselves thin by joining numerous organizations, at the expense of their academics. My colleagues and I call this *"majoring in the minors."* You join every organization that you can, in an attempt to build your resume, meet people, and enjoy the college experience. However, your grades suffer, because you spend less time on your studies and more time on practice, rehearsals, meetings, and other events.

There is something that every student should realize about these organizations. They mean absolutely *nothing* if you don't have a degree. The purpose of you attending college is to earn a degree, not join 15 organizations. I've seen one too many students go on academic probation and even suspension as a result of this. Some were students who had scholarships and were excelling academically. Unfortunately, their commitment to on-campus organizations significantly outweighed their commitment to their studies. Remember, your studies are your priority. Anything else you do is in *moderation.* In chapter 4, we discussed time management. Only participate in those activities and organizations that fit within those available "non-essential" times in your schedule.

You Are Not Alone

Even though it may feel like it at times, you are *never* alone. Lean on that positive group of individuals that you have surrounded yourself with, including family, friends (old and new), professors, mentors, and others. You have a support system, whether you realize it or not. Use it to get through any obstacles and help celebrate your victories.

Lean on Your Home Team

Whether it's a former teacher, guidance counselor, mentor, family member, or friend of the family, utilize the people around you. Whether you realize it or not, there is someone that can provide help with anything you encounter or experience. Do not be afraid to actively seek them out. They want you to be successful.

Step Ten

Take Care of Your Physical and Mental Health

You only have one body. How well you take care of it will determine how it responds as you age. You may not think this is something that you need to worry about right now. After all, you are young and in pretty good health, right? Just remember, the young do age. When this happens, you want to look and feel as good as possible. I've witnessed plenty of young adults ignore their physical and mental health, often suffering the consequences much sooner than anticipated.

While it's important to take care of your physical, mental, and emotional health during your college years, it's also important to continue this throughout the rest of your life. The topics discussed in this chapter do not apply to just your college years. Begin making these a permanent part of your routine. It has been said that it takes approximately 30 days to form a habit. Consider this day 1.

Disclaimer: I am not a medical doctor nor do I claim to be. My advice is based on my own experience and observations of those around me, including peers and students.

Maintaining Physical Health

Have you heard of the "freshman 15?" This refers to the significant amount of weight that some undergraduates gain in their first year of college. Your weight is only one factor affecting your physical health. The advice below is designed to help you improve and maintain your overall physical health, both inside and out.

1. *Get enough sleep.* What constitutes "enough" sleep depends on you. You know your body. On the days that you have felt the best waking up, and been the most

productive, how many hours of sleep did you get? I have no problem admitting that I love to sleep. In fact, the only thing I love more than sleeping is eating. If I could sleep 10-11 hours a night I would. I've always been that way (and it's one of the reasons I absolutely love my career, since I don't have to wake up early every day). I realize though that sleeping that many hours daily does not make me very productive. My "sweet spot" is somewhere around 8 hours. If I exercise and am in good physical shape, I may be able to shave an hour or two off of that. Whatever your body requires, get the rest you need.

2. *Develop and maintain an exercise routine.* Physical fitness is good not only for your body, but also your mind. If you don't have an exercise routine, dedicate 30 minutes three to four days a week to some physical activity. As you become comfortable with this routine, increase the time as you can. You will find that you not only feel better, but also look and sleep better. You will also have more energy than you did before. Exercise has always been a great tool for clearing my mind. I often found that a problem I couldn't solve became much simpler after exercising. Any stress disappeared too. Most colleges and universities have facilities on campus that are free for students to use (e.g. gymnasium, pool, exercise room, track, etc.). If you aren't comfortable exercising alone, find a friend to join you. In addition, try to mix things up. Do different things, and try new adventures. Whatever you choose, commit to it. Your body and mind will thank you!

3. *Develop and maintain proper eating habits.* We are a "microwave" or "fast-food" society. We want everything now, in a hurry. This includes our meals. How many times have you gone to a fast-food restaurant, because you felt like you didn't have enough time to have a "real meal?" As a college student, you may find yourself eating fast food more times than you can count. After all, you're studying and doing 15 other things in a day. You

don't have time to cook or eat healthy, right? *WRONG!* Despite your hectic schedule, make sure you eat properly. Remember, you may not feel any effects now. But too much of this has a number of negative effects. Make sure you eat three balanced meals per day. I confess, I don't always eat breakfast. I'm not a morning person, so I'm often rushing to get dressed and get out the door. However, I've learned to grab fruit and other things that I can at least take with me. In addition, I've also learned to *slow down*! Take 10-15 minutes to eat something in the mornings. Think of how effective you are in class and studies when you skip breakfast. Not too productive, right? Also monitor what you eat. I know it can be difficult when you are in the dining hall and there is so much food available (and usually buffet style). Just remember moderation. Also, keep healthy snacks to eat between meals. These can include fruit and nuts. Finally, I urge you to stay away from things like energy pills and drinks. I have seen a number of students take these to complete a project due the next day or study for an exam. I do not support these at all. If you need rest, get some. It's just that simple.

4. *Drink plenty of water.* I confess. I don't always drink water like I should. As a southern girl, I love Pepsi and sweet tea. I have to make a conscious effort to drink water throughout the day. I don't drink 8-10 glasses per day. However, I drink water. And for every Pepsi or tea I have, I drink at least two glasses of water to make up for it. Suffice it to say I don't drink as much caffeine anymore. Whatever you have to do to get your water intake, find something that works for you.

5. *Get regular medical checkups.* Make sure you get regular medical, dental, and specialist checkups as needed. As college students, most of you are still on your parents' health insurance. Every college and university has a student health center, if not a hospital. If you have any prescribed medicine, make sure you follow the

dosage instructions. If you require prescription refills, do this in a timely manner so that you do not miss any doses.

6. *Pay attention to your body.* If something doesn't feel right, seek medical advice. *DO NOT* self-diagnose. Leave this to the experts. This is especially important for students who have medical conditions. Some of my students have been epileptic, diabetic, and more. I usually learned this after something happened to them as a result of not taking their medicine or taking care of themselves. You know what you must do to maintain your health. Follow these directions, take all prescribed medicines as instructed, get plenty of rest, and watch your eating habits. These are especially important for you, as your condition can be affected by any of these factors and more.

7. *Seek medical attention when needed.* Don't ignore any signs your body gives you. Again, you are not a medical doctor. Take care of yourself as much as you can. However, when necessary, go to the doctor, urgent care, or emergency room if necessary. The longer you ignore something, the worse it becomes. You know your body, so heed the warning signs and act accordingly. Remember, you only have one body and one life. Take care of it.

8. *Use protection...ALWAYS.* Some may not like or want to read this, but let's be honest. Sex is happening on college campuses. The reality is that many of you will be faced with decisions to make regarding your sexual lifestyle. If you choose to engage in any activity, be smart. Always use contraceptives. Sexually transmitted diseases (STD's) are a serious issue, especially on college campuses. Protect yourself at *all* times. I am not advocating that you participate in or abstain from sex. What I *am* advocating is that you protect yourself at all times and don't allow your emotions or peer pressure to influence you to make bad decisions. This goes for males

and females. Remember, *no one* will fight for you except you. Force people to respect your wishes. I tell my students who ask for advice, if you want to act like adults when you are on the yard, you need to discuss and handle situations like an adult. Also get tested for STD's and require it of your partners. *NEVER* allow someone to tell you that you should "trust them." Remember, you cannot tell by looking at a person if they have an STD or not.

9. *Avoid any and all drugs not prescribed to you by a medical doctor.* Again, I'm being honest. Some students experiment with drugs while in college. Unless it was prescribed to you, do *NOT* use it. In addition to actual drugs, there are so many household products being used as drugs now. Again, you have *NO* idea how these things will affect you. Think about your family, and the fact that they have trusted you to conduct yourself as a responsible young adult for the first time in your life. Do you really want to let them down by doing such a stupid thing? You are in college to get an education. If there is something you are not comfortable with your parents, professors, or religious leaders witnessing, then chances are you shouldn't be doing it.

10. *Do not drink alcohol if under the age of 21.* At some point, you will probably have access to things you didn't before, including alcohol. Most college campuses are dry. This means that alcohol or consumption is prohibited. Somehow though, it makes its way into a few dorm rooms. I know of a few incidents where students were caught with multiple bottles in their dorm rooms. This is a serious offense. Not only are you not of legal age but, you can also be expelled. Just like rules, laws are in place for specific reasons. College is not the time to test these boundaries. Wait until you are 21.

11. *Do NOT drink and drive.* Don't be stupid. If you drink, give someone else (who is sober) your keys to drive you, call a cab or organization that serves as designated

drivers, or take the bus or metro. *NEVER* get in the car with a driver who has been drinking. If you are sober, take the keys and drive. If not, then find an alternate method for getting home. There are too many accidents each year due to drunk driving. These are accidents that can easily be avoided by simply not drinking and driving. Simply put, *DON'T DO IT*. Be smart.

12. *Drink responsibly.* I sometimes wonder if there is a sense of invincibility that is felt as a college student. I know that, during my time in college, I felt somewhat insulated from the outside world. Certain things that happened in "the real world" weren't even on my radar. I was very naïve. I'm sure I'm not the only person who thought this way. In fact, I know I'm not the only one, because there are always news reports that seem to illustrate this mindset. How many times have you heard news reports about binge drinking on college campuses? Whether it's a party, so-called initiation process, or basic peer pressure, it's important to realize that the consumption of alcohol can significantly impact your body and life. Every year, there is a story about a student who died from binge drinking. Again, don't be stupid.

Maintaining Emotional/Mental Health

College is supposed to be an amazing time in your life. It should be fun, challenging, and enjoyable. This is your first introduction to "the real world." Though it's not quite as accurate as the real thing, you will be expected to develop not only discipline-specific skills to help you navigate through your career, but also personal and interpersonal skills that will help you to navigate through life. This includes learning to handle pressure, disappointment, and failure in school, relationships, family, and life in general.

Your emotional/mental health is just as important as your physical health. There are so many things that can impact it, and a major part of successfully completing college (and having a ball doing it) includes a good balance of both. Over my career,

I've met students who've dealt with issues in their personal lives that I couldn't have imagined dealing with at their age. Some were able to persevere and graduate. Others weren't so fortunate. Hopefully you will take the lessons in this chapter and apply them to ensure your success. Many of the steps discussed under physical health apply to your mental health as well. You should also include the suggestions below:

1. *Find daily "me" time.* There are so many things that you have to do in one day that, it's easy to become overwhelmed. One of the best things I learned as a student was how to mentally "check out" for a while. There are those moments when a project isn't coming together as expected, I can't solve a problem, and something is going on in my personal life. During these times, I stop what I'm doing and take a breather. I learned this from my graduate school advisor. I would be so overwhelmed with things as a type-A personality, and he was so laid back and easy going. He loved to go sailing. He would often take a week and sail during the middle of the semester. I learned to take breaks as well. Sometimes that time away allowed me to view the work differently when I returned. Each day, you should find some personal time. This may be dedicated to exercise, meditation, prayer, reading, cooking, watching television, listening to music, or silence.

2. *Talk to someone.* One of the biggest mistakes you can make is trying to handle all of your problems alone. You can easily and unnecessarily overwhelm yourself. Speak to a mentor, faculty, or staff member you trust. A good professor can identify that something is different in a student. I've had numerous students who seemed to completely change direction in terms of their academic performance. When I spoke with them privately, I learned that there were issues ranging from parents divorcing, relationships ending, financial strains, pregnancy, and illness. Whatever it is, let someone know if you feel overwhelmed. Do not be afraid to ask for help.

If you need to speak to a mental health professional, then let your parents know as well. Most universities offer support services for students. Identify these and any counseling options that are available.

3. *Eliminate toxic things and people.* These are unnecessary drains on you mentally. It should be self-explanatory why you do not need this in your life.

4. *Make you a priority.* With balancing studies, organizations, and other commitments in your life, it can be very easy to forget about you. What good are you to anyone and anything if you aren't at your best? Remember, no one will fight for you except you. Make yourself a priority *EVERY* day.

Final Thoughts
Your Professors Want You to Know...

By now, you should have a pretty good idea of how to have the most successful, enjoyable, and memorable college experience possible. It really is the best years of your life, if done right. The key to this is knowing the expectations, the obstacles you could possibly face, and how to best avoid or overcome them.

At this point, the only things I have left to share with you are things that I randomly share with students in my classes, programs, or conversation. I always wondered, as a college student, what my professors thought or said about my classmates and me. Were they annoyed that half of the class fell asleep during the lecture or didn't turn in an assignment? Did they laugh at some of ridiculous questions and answers provided by students? Did they know when we didn't read or study? Did they dread coming to that 8am class as much as we did?

I finally learned when I became a professor that the answer to each of these is *ABSOLUTELY*! So just in case you're wondering, here are a few other things we professors wish you would realize, and quickly:

1. *The grade you receive is the grade you earn.* I cannot stand hearing "Dr. Washington *gave* me a D." I quickly correct anyone stating this with "no, you *earned* that D." I don't give grades. I merely track the performance of each student throughout the course and enter that info into the appropriate university system. Translation: if you want an A or B, then you need to do the work to earn it. Remember the five P's: prior preparation prevents poor performance.

2. *No one is going to hold your hand.* Again, this isn't high school. We aren't going to beg you to do your work. We expect that, since you took the time to apply to and attend college, you have some level of concern about your academic future. In addition, we aren't going to call home to keep your parents abreast of your progress. This is your responsibility. Act accordingly.

3. *Every closed eye ain't sleep.* My grandmother used to tell me this all the time. Translation: we see what you're doing not only inside but also outside of the classroom. How you conduct yourself on the yard can impact faculty, staff, and administrator's views of you. Remember, you need recommendations, references, and more.

4. *If you act like an adult on the yard, we expect you to do the same in the classroom.* We see what you do outside of class, specifically how "adult-like" you conduct yourself when around your friends or with your significant others. We see how you love to take initiative to organize a social event in the department or school. We expect you to take the same initiative in the classroom. "I don't know how to do this" is an insufficient response. Attempt to solve any problem, find your stopping point, and be able to articulate your need, which leads to the next point.

5. *Look the part.* I have a dress code policy in my class. Young men are not allowed to wear hats in class. No one is allowed to wear revealing or obscene clothing. The reason is simple. You are here to learn and in life, there is a time and place for everything. I've long debated with friends and colleagues about why I have such a policy in my class. The fact remains that, while computer science isn't a suit-and-tie discipline, you need to be able to present yourself well, should the need arise. This means taking pride in your personal appearance. If you interview with prospective employers, you must look

presentable. For those of you with entrepreneurial ambitions, remember that you may still have to present to investors or others who are paying attention to your appearance. Not only should you dress the part, but practice your presentation, speaking, and writing skills.

6. *We really wish you would stop majoring in the minors.* This reminds me of the movie "Groundhog's Day," where Bill Murray woke up every day, and the exact same events happened over and over again. Every year a new class of students enters the university. Every year, we warn that class (and the other returning students) to focus on studies and do everything in moderation. Every year, there are students who don't listen, think they are different, and end up repeating history. Do yourself a favor and heed our warning. After all, we witness this every year…every…single…year.

7. *No one will fight for you like you.* Don't become complacent. Remember that you have to not only hold yourself, but those at the university accountable. I've talked to students about issues that involved less than acceptable living conditions, professors who never showed for class for the majority of the semester, and other issues around campus. When asked what they've done to address this problem, sadly most respond not much. Remember, you are the customer. You are the reason we are all here. We can't fight these battles for you. These are the important things you *should* be standing up for. Arguing us down after the final exam about why we should allow you to make up assignments you chose not to complete all semester (so you can pass the class) is not a valid fight. Pick your battles wisely.

8. *You aren't the only big fish in this pond.* There was a lyric in a song by DMX that said "everybody is the man, in their own hood." Translation: you are surrounded by students from across the world, many of whom were one of the top students from their high school. You are no

longer the only or one of the few superstars on campus. There is *always* someone smarter than you. Humility will get you much further than arrogance.

9. *There are no dumb questions (other than how can I change my grade).* Many students are afraid to ask questions in class because they don't want to appear stupid. Don't believe the hype. The truth is that you aren't alone. There are usually several students who want to ask the same question, but are just as scared to open their mouth.

10. *We really aren't stupid.* We've heard all the excuses before. Your computer crashed, your car broke down, or you had a sudden, 24-hour onset of this life-threatening sickness that caused you to miss an assignment, exam, or class. The best excuse I've received to date was the student who emailed me 30 minutes into the midterm exam to inform me that he overslept and wouldn't be able to make the exam, so could I please allow him to make it up. If I could grade based on entertainment, he would've definitely received an A+. Sadly, I can't. I just can't.

11. *Relationships will come and go.* Not everyone you date in college is "the one." Be smart in your dating decisions, involve yourself with individuals who complement you and will help you reach all of your goals. You should also provide the same to them. Anyone who deters you from your studies is not a person you should be dating. Remember who should be in your "five." I'm not saying you can't or won't meet your future husband or wife. After all, my parents were college sweethearts, and many of their friends were. Dating is entirely different than it was when they were in college though. Ladies, remember that you are not in college to get an "M-R-S." That means you didn't come to college to find a husband. Gentlemen, remember that each young woman you meet deserves your respect. If you happen to meet your future

husband/wife, then congratulations! If not, it's completely ok. You will have plenty of time to find your soul mate when you graduate.

12. *Posting online is like writing in ink.* Translation: you can't erase it. Pictures and videos you post online don't disappear just because you deleted them. Trust me. I'm a computer science professor. We warn students about the implications of inappropriate use of social media daily. What you post on online can come back to haunt you. Employers and colleges now check applicant's social networking footprint, to ensure there is no inappropriate information there. In addition, some individuals have been terminated from their job due to inappropriate comments, images, or videos posted online. Other students have lost scholarships because of offensive information they posted online. To circumvent this, do yourself a favor and use social networking in a professional and appropriate manner. You can have fun with friends. However, keep it classy. Remember, every closed eye ain't sleep.

13. *Stay current.* Your knowledge should expand beyond your courses, major, and campus. Know what's going on in the world. Technology affords you 24-hour access to news across the world. You may be questioned on current events in an interview. In addition, it helps you understand how your major, degree, and career aspirations can help you compete in a global economy. Do not simply rely on blogs and television for your information. Read the newspaper. Yes, this may seem antiquated. However, reading newspapers, magazines, and journals helps you expand your vocabulary while expanding your knowledge. You can access many of these mediums online, if you don't have access to the print version.

14. *Take one computer science course before you graduate.* This is the one discipline that has more jobs than

qualified graduates to fill them. As society becomes more technology dependent, it is almost mandatory that you have some basic level of computer skills prior to graduation. Regardless of your major, enroll in an introductory programming course. This will teach you problem solving, computational thinking, logic, and more. These are skills that bridge numerous disciplines and are extremely valuable in the workforce.

www.ingramcontent.com/pod-product-compliance
Lightning Source LLC
Chambersburg PA
CBHW051456290426
44109CB00016B/1779